BY VED MEHTA

Face to Face

Walking the Indian Streets

Fly and the Fly-Bottle

The New Theologian

Delinquent Chacha

Portrait of India

John Is Easy to Please

Mahatma Gandhi and His Apostles

The New India

The Photographs of Chachaji

A Family Affair

Three Stories of the Raj

Rajiv Gandhi and Rama's Kingdom

CONTINENTS OF EXILE

Daddyji

Mamaji

Vedi

The Ledge Between the Streams

Sound-Shadows of the New World

The Stolen Light

Up at Oxford

RAJIV GANDHI

and

Rama's Kingdom

Rajiv and Jawaharlal Nehru. New Delhi. Nehru's birthday, ca. 1960.
(P. D. Tandon, from Teen Murthi Collection.)

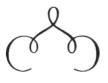

RAJIV GANDHI

and

Rama's Kingdom

VED MEHTA

YALE UNIVERSITY PRESS
New Haven and London

The contents of this book originally appeared in *The New Yorker* in somewhat different form, with the exception of the last chapter, part of which was first published in *Foreign Affairs*.

Typeset by The Composing Room of Michigan, Inc.
Printed in the United States of America.

Library of Congress Cataloging-in-Publication Data

Mehta, Ved, 1934–
Rajiv Gandhi and Rama's kingdom / Ved Mehta.
p.   cm.
Includes index.
Continues: A family affair.
ISBN 0-300-06038-6 (alk. paper)
1. India—Politics and government—1977–.   2. Gandhi, Rajiv,
1944–1991.   I. Mehta, Ved, 1934–   Family affair.
DS480.853.M432   1994
954.05′2′092—dc20   94-15420
CIP

A catalogue record for this book is available from the British Library.

The paper in this book meets the guidelines for permanence and durability of the Committee on Production Guidelines for Book Longevity of the Council on Library Resources.

10 9 8 7 6 5 4 3 2 1

TO HENRY AND MARY COOPER

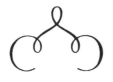

Contents

PREFACE   xi

• 1 •

The Democratic Monarchy   1

• 2 •

The Turban and the Cap   35

• 3 •

Rajiv's Political Honeymoon   61

• 4 •

The Greatest Factory-Based Accident   85

• 5 •

The Divorced Muslim Woman   93

· 6 ·

The Telephone Exchange Caper   101

· 7 ·

Rajiv's Perestroika   115

· 8 ·

The Assassination and the General Election   143

· 9 ·

The Mosque and Rama's Kingdom   169

INDEX   189

PREFACE

In 1965, I proposed a piece on India, the country of my birth, to William Shawn, the editor of *The New Yorker*. I had been living in America and England for seventeen years and, for economic reasons, had not been able to make more than one brief visit home. He said that since I had family there and would enjoy a visit home he would O.K. the piece, but that he could not justify sending me there on strictly professional grounds, for *The New Yorker* had no need to cover India the way it covered France, for instance. I couldn't bring myself to ask him if he would consider paying my airfare. I had written for *The New Yorker* for six years and had talked to him about everything under the sun except money. I now realize that I had come to share his unspoken assumption that good writing is a vocation, which has its origins in passion and dedication, and had therefore concluded that any mention of money would somehow debase the enterprise. In any event, I knew that an O.K. from William Shawn was an expression of support and confidence without any conditions, so I used my savings to spend six months travelling through India. I then spent three or four years in New York recollecting my experiences and deepening them with reading and reflection. As a result, my piece on India turned out to be nine long pieces, which appeared in *The New Yorker* over a period of three years and were published in book form in 1970 as "Portrait of

India." (The book was reissued in 1993.) I have since made regular visits to India, and have written reports on my observations of the country and on my conversations, readings, and meditations concerning it—reports that have appeared in *The New Yorker* every year or two under the rubric "Letter from New Delhi." The reports written between 1974 and 1981 became the basis of two books on Indian politics—"The New India" (1978) and "A Family Affair" (1982). "Rajiv Gandhi and Rama's Kingdom" is the third in this series. Perhaps I should add that my intent as I went over the reports with a view to publishing them in book form was not to bring out collections but, rather, to transform the reports into analytic narratives—a task that turned out to be fairly straightforward, since they were originally written as probing stories. Now, in my mind, at least, the three books, taken together, constitute an informal journal of political events in New Delhi—and, by extension, in India—over the last twenty years or so, and, together with "Portrait," the journal has consistently had two purposes: to explain India to myself and to people generally.

In the ten years this book was in the making—in between the writing of five other books—I was assisted by several people in the preparation of a section here, a section there. I give my warm, lasting thanks to them; to Elizabeth Wagner, for her help with the final push to finish the book; to Salman Haidar, for his comments on an early draft of the manuscript (with, of course, the caveat that responsibility for the text is mine and mine alone); and, for help as unutterable as love, to my wife, Linn, to Eleanor Gould Packard, and to William Shawn, who, to my great sorrow, did not live to see the book in its final form.

V.M.
New York
January, 1994

RAJIV GANDHI

and

Rama's Kingdom

1

The Democratic Monarchy

On the early afternoon of March 29, 1982, Prime Minister Indira
Gandhi summoned to her office in the Prime Minister's house—
her government residence—in New Delhi her daughter-in-law
Maneka, who had been widowed less than two years earlier, at the
age of twenty-three, when Mrs. Gandhi's younger son, Sanjay, died
in the crash of a sports plane he was flying. Maneka had lived with
Mrs. Gandhi for seven years, ever since she married Sanjay, but now
Mrs. Gandhi peremptorily told her that she must quit the house
immediately.

"What have I done?" Maneka asked. "I have already explained
everything to you."

"You have attended the convention, and now you face the
consequences!" Mrs. Gandhi shouted. The convention in question
had been held the day before by a few of Sanjay's disgruntled
followers. Mrs. Gandhi had made it known that she considered the
convention subversive to her rule. Maneka had attended it, claiming that its purpose was only to honor Sanjay's memory and promote his work. (My account of the events of that day is based on
what newspaper reporters overheard at the Prime Minister's house,
on their interviews with eyewitnesses, and on published letters and
statements from the participants.)

In the office with her, Mrs. Gandhi had two men who were

among her closest aides—R. K. Dhawan, her longtime private secretary, and Dhirendra Brahmachari (Dhirendra the Celibate), her strong-armed yoga instructor—and they seemed to be simply waiting to escort Maneka from the house.

At one point, Maneka begged two days' grace, pointing out that she needed time to pack and to find a place to live. Mrs. Gandhi said that she could go and live with her mother. Maneka's mother, Amteshwar Anand, had a house of her own in New Delhi.

Maneka packed, and the servants carried the luggage to a truck waiting outside. Dhawan and Brahmachari stopped them: they wanted to open and search the bags. Maneka protested, and Mrs. Gandhi rushed out of her private room to take the side of her aides. But Maneka got her way about the luggage: without being opened, it was carried out, in full view of reporters, guards, and drivers, and loaded on the truck.

Maneka then asked that her two-year-old son, Varun (short for Feroze Varuna), who was in Mrs. Gandhi's room, be brought to her.

"No," Mrs. Gandhi said, and she started crying. Since she lost Sanjay, she had generally had Varun sleep in her room.

Maneka said that if she couldn't take Varun she would squat outside the house in civil disobedience.

Mrs. Gandhi ran back into her room.

It was now four-fifteen. Maneka remained in the house while Dhawan and others spent several hours talking with police and lawyers to see if there was some legal way that Mrs. Gandhi could keep the grandson without his mother. They were told not: all that Maneka would have to do was to go to a police station and lodge a complaint against Mrs. Gandhi, and Varun would have to be restored to her.

Around six, Maneka's two prized dogs, Bruno and Sheba, were driven across to Mrs. Anand's house. Around seven-thirty, Maneka's luggage was taken there. Around eight-thirty, Mrs. Gandhi's surviving son, Rajiv, who had kept out of the row, took Varun's toys there. All the while, Mrs. Gandhi and Maneka, in different rooms, continued their row by proxy—aides and servants carrying messages back and forth.

One source of the row between the mother-in-law and the daughter-in-law was dissension that had arisen between Mrs. Gandhi and Mrs. Anand, who were very different in character and personality. In manner, Mrs. Gandhi was ordinarily aristocratic and aloof, while Mrs. Anand was rustic and talkative; Mrs. Gandhi was referred to in newspapers and in drawing rooms in New Delhi as "the iron lady" and "a man among women," while Mrs. Anand was referred to as "a social butterfly" and "a merry widow." (Maneka herself had the reputation of being something of a free spirit. As a teen-ager, she had dropped out of college and dabbled in modelling for a towel company and a mattress company, and in journalism. Then, at seventeen, she had met Sanjay, and, counter to the almost universal Indian custom of arranged marriages, they had made a "love marriage.") Maneka's father, Lieutenant Colonel T. S. Anand, was shot dead in early June, 1977, soon after the Janata Party defeated Mrs. Gandhi at the polls and came to power. A few adherents of fanciful conspiracy theories claimed that Sanjay had had him killed, out of fear that his father-in-law would be an undependable witness in various cases that the Janata government was pressing against Sanjay. (The cases concerned Sanjay's conduct during the Emergency—that period between 1975 and 1977 when Mrs. Gandhi assumed dictatorial powers, and Sanjay, who had not then been elected to any office, functioned as the unofficial crown prince.) But almost everybody believed that the colonel had become so despondent over the legal plight of his son-in-law that he killed himself. In any event, Mrs. Anand was reported to feel that she had lost her husband to Sanjay's cause. Soon after Sanjay's death, in June, 1980, she asked Mrs. Gandhi to make Maneka—perhaps as reparation— the president of the youth wing of the Congress Indira Party. (The Indian National Congress Party had had two splits—one, in 1969, into the Old Congress Party and the Congress Party, and the other, in 1978, into the Official Congress Party and the Congress Indira.

The Old Congress and the Official Congress remained small, splinter parties, while the Congress and eventually its successor, the Congress Indira, became the ruling party.) That was the position that Sanjay had used as his political base. Mrs. Gandhi turned her down, saying that Maneka could not be so "catapulted." (People around Mrs. Gandhi referred to Maneka as "a political twit.") Then both Mrs. Anand and Maneka agitated for a role in the choice of a Congress Indira candidate from the parliamentary constituency of Amethi, in Uttar Pradesh; Sanjay had been elected to Parliament from Amethi in January, 1980, and the Party had not yet nominated anyone for his vacant seat. Mrs. Gandhi demurred. She wanted the seat to go to Rajiv, although Rajiv had never taken any part in politics; he was a career pilot for Indian Airlines, the government-owned domestic carrier, and he was married to a foreigner (an Italian, Sonia Maino)—something that was generally considered an insurmountable political obstacle. In the end, Rajiv was given the Party nomination, and he was elected to Sanjay's seat in 1981. Around that time, Mrs. Gandhi barred Mrs. Anand from the Prime Minister's house. (It had been Mrs. Anand's custom to go there daily to see Maneka and to play with Varun.) Mrs. Gandhi said that Maneka should go and see her mother at her mother's house, and ordered that Varun should be taken there every afternoon.

After Sanjay's death, Maneka had found herself increasingly isolated in the Prime Minister's house. She was twenty-three, yet, by Indian custom, she couldn't move about the city freely, she couldn't go out and see anyone she chose. She was the daughter-in-law of an embattled Prime Minister, and she was a Hindu widow. (In Hinduism, widows have a low status. Although Maneka probably didn't suffer any formal disabilities on account of her widowhood, still she was beholden to Mrs. Gandhi.) Her contacts were confined to a handful of friends who could be received in the Prime Minister's house. She had many grievances, real or imagined. (When Mrs. Gandhi and members of her family went on a trip to Nairobi in 1981, Maneka was said to have taken umbrage at the fact that Rajiv's children, Rahul and Priyanka, had gone on a diplomatic passport, like Mrs. Gandhi, while she herself had to go on an ordinary passport, like that of the ayah accompanying the children.) In the meantime, Rajiv's kite was climbing higher and higher, although, as S. Nihal Singh, who was the former editor-in-chief of the *Indian Express,* the most widely read English-language daily, noted in the summer of 1982, "it is a sad fact that since his formal entry into politics, Rajiv has failed to impress." After winning his seat, he had at first brushed aside the suggestion that he might one day succeed his mother, but soon he had started talking about the succession as thinkable; to a New York *Times* reporter he acknowledged, "Well, yes, the heritage can be passed."

In February of 1982, in what many in New Delhi called "Mrs. Anand's revenge on Mrs. Gandhi," Mrs. Anand secretly sold for an undisclosed price the monthly magazine *Surya* ("Sun"), which had come to be associated with the name and the memory of Sanjay. Mrs. Anand and Maneka had started the magazine during the Emergency and had successfully financed it through the high-pressure tactics of Indian politics—cajoling friends and business-men to advertise in it in return for political favors. But after San-jay's death it had begun losing money—from fifteen to twenty thousand rupees a month (in that period the rupee was fluctuating between eight and ten to the dollar)—partly because all magazines were down but mostly because without Sanjay the magazine had no political clout. Mrs. Gandhi was offended: not only had the sale been consummated behind her back but Sanjay's magazine had gone to two hated enemies of hers. The magazine's new owners—Dr. Janendra Kumar Jain and Sardar Sambhaji Chandroji Angre—had connections with two opposition organizations: the right-wing Hindu-chauvinist Rashtriya Swayamsevak Sangh (National Volunteer Force), or R.S.S., and the Janata remnant, the Bharatiya Janata Party (Indian People's Party). Worse still, Angre was the private secretary and confidant of Rajmata Vijaya Raje Scindia, the former queen mother of the former princely state of Gwalior, who had stood against Mrs. Gandhi in the 1980 elections—a campaign characterized by bitter personal attacks—and who was the vice-president of the Bharatiya Janata Party. (As it happened, Mrs. Scindia was embroiled in a public feud with her son Madhavrao, the former Maharaja of Gwalior, over Angre's influence on her. Madhavrao was an important member of Congress Indira, so the loss of *Surya* to Angre in particular was additionally galling to Mrs. Gandhi.) Maneka denied all knowledge of the secret sale, but Mrs. Gandhi refused to believe her, because Maneka was very close to her mother, and because Mrs. Scindia's younger daughter, Vasundhara, was Maneka's best friend and was in and out of the Prime Minister's house. In fact, Mrs. Gandhi felt that the shady dealings with her foes might have been carried on under her own roof. She felt compromised and betrayed.

Jain and Angre publicly gloated that they had scored a palace coup and that Mrs. Gandhi would not be able to ignore it. In two sensational articles that Jain wrote for *Surya*—entitled "The Writing on the Wall" and "Was There a Plot to Murder Maneka?"—he reported that soon after he acquired the magazine the Prime Minister's household tried to buy it back. He said that he was summoned to the Prime Minister's house, and was received there by Brahmachari and by Maneka and Vasundhara. (The reason for the two women's involvement—whether it was only for a show of unity with Mrs. Gandhi or out of a real interest in trying to recover the magazine—Jain didn't make clear.) He wrote that Brahmachari bullied him for an hour to get him to sell the magazine to them, saying that money was no object, and even offering him and Angre seats in the upper house of Parliament. (The Prime Minister nominates certain members of the upper house.) Jain said he refused. The next day, he said, he received an offer of two and a half million rupees—perhaps a hundred times what he had paid for the magazine—from a supposed emissary of the Prime Minister, but he declined it and declared that he would negotiate only with the principal, the Prime Minister herself. According to Jain, the good offices of another intermediary were then sought—Mrs. Gandhi talked to a Hindu holy woman, the late Anandamayi Ma, who, in turn, talked to Maneka, who, in turn, talked to Jain—but nothing came of this effort. Jain also reported that there were rumors of a plot by the Prime Minister's household to murder Maneka. The accuracy of Jain's reporting is impossible to check, but Maneka confirmed some of the details, and Jain's broad sketch of events was generally accepted in New Delhi.

Just after the sale of *Surya*, Mrs. Gandhi was informed that, in defiance of her wishes and those of her party, Akbar Ahmed, known to one and all as Dumpy, was calling that fateful convention. The convention was to be of the Uttar Pradesh youth branch of Congress Indira on March 28th in Lucknow, the state's capital. Dumpy was a Congress Indira member of the Uttar Pradesh legislative assembly. A contemporary of Sanjay's, he had been his intimate; in fact, the families of the two young men had been close for most of this century. Dumpy was also a close friend of Maneka and Vasundhara. He announced that he hoped that the Lucknow convention would give new direction and encouragement to leaderless Sanjay men, and claimed that Maneka had agreed to inaugurate it. The calling of the convention was immediately seen by political observers as an anti–Mrs. Gandhi, anti-Party, and, above all, anti-Rajiv act. Rajiv had no use for most of Sanjay's brash friends and associates, who, like Dumpy, had come to power on Sanjay's coattails in national or state politics in the 1980 elections. He was at pains to dissociate himself from them and from Sanjay's rough-and-ready methods. Over the months, many of the Sanjay men had settled down into a subservient place in the rank and file of Congress Indira. Some of them, however, remained restive, longing for the influence of the Sanjay days and fearing that the Rajiv men would not give them Party nominations for the next general election. Dumpy was one of these disgruntled Sanjay men, and, like others, he hoped to make Maneka a rallying point for a center of power to rival Rajiv's.

Congress Indira in Uttar Pradesh at once suspended Dumpy from the Party, in an attempt to hold other Party legislators in line. The Party ruled the state, but the state politics were turbulent, and there was always a chance that large-scale defections in the name of Sanjay and Maneka could impair, perhaps even topple, the state government. Maneka, however, would neither confirm nor deny that she planned to attend the Lucknow convention. Then, on March 25th, while Mrs. Gandhi was in London for the Festival of India, Maneka quietly went in a car to Corbett Park, an animal sanctuary close to the city of Moradabad, near Delhi, with Varun, her brother Viren, and a couple of friends. She was an animal enthusiast, and her trip had the appearance of a private outing, but in Moradabad she secretly met Dumpy and dispatched a letter to Mrs. Gandhi. (Apparently, its contents were immediately communicated to her in London.) "I thought you would tell me what to do or at least help me reach a decision," she wrote, "but since you didn't say anything, I came to Corbett Park to think it out on my own." She added, "Please don't get angry as I am really doing this to nip any possible mischief in the bud. A lot of peculiar attitudes have arisen in the last few weeks—mainly due to intermediaries and the press—and I hope the 28th will sort everything out."

Mrs. Gandhi returned on the afternoon of the twenty-seventh, and at a press conference at the airport she said of the Lucknow convention, "It is obvious to all Party members that it is an anti-Party act, because it has been encouraged by those who are against us and against me—R.S.S., B.J.P. Many of the people who are now encouraging the convention and are behind it financially and otherwise are the very people who were against Sanjay." That evening, Maneka arrived in Lucknow in a car, and the organizers of the convention cheered her in the streets. Loyal members of the Party stoned her car. The next day, when she was due to open the convention, a letter from Mrs. Gandhi was hand-delivered to her at noon at the hotel in which she was staying. The letter said that Maneka had to choose between her and the convention—that if she attended it the doors of the Prime Minister's house would be forever closed to her. Maneka went to the convention.

The convention was held in a small hall, which was decorated with posters exhibiting photographs of Maneka, Mrs. Gandhi, and Sanjay, and such slogans as "Long live Mrs. Gandhi!" and "Sanjay is immortal." The spectators, who all sat on the floor, numbered at most two thousand; many village rallies draw bigger crowds. There were only a few defecting legislators. Maneka spoke for ten minutes. "I express my gratitude to you from the depths of my heart for organizing this program," she said, and tried to dissociate herself from the R.S.S. and the Jana Sangh. The R.S.S., founded in 1925, was a paramilitary group that was ostensibly non-political but was linked to the right-wing Hindu Jana Sangh Party. Indeed, the Jana Sangh had come into being as a political arm of the R.S.S., which thereafter was sometimes referred to as the Jana Sangh's Brown Shirts. The Jana Sangh was a constituent of the Janata Party, a coalition of most of the major non-Communist opposition parties, and the Janata government had pressed many cases against the Gandhi family. Maneka said things like "I am R.S.S. or something, this I have heard for the first time. The wife of Sanjay Gandhi who fought the Janata Party at every footstep and who had eleven cases against her, how can she join hands with R.S.S.?" and "I shall always honor the discipline and reputation of the great Nehru-Gandhi family I belong to," and "As my husband proved that the cases against him were baseless, I, too, take a vow in the same manner that all of us should further strengthen the hands of the Prime Minister in this hour." The convention decided to start a national organization, with a branch in every state, to be known as Sanjay's Five-Point Forum. (During the Emergency, Sanjay had initiated a Four-Point Program—for the control of population growth, the beautification of the countryside, the extension of literacy, and the abolition of the dowry. Later, beautification had been divided into slum clearance and tree planting, and the Four-Point Program had become the Five-Point Program.)

It was on the day following the convention that Mrs. Gandhi ordered Maneka to quit the Prime Minister's house. Around nine that evening, some time after Maneka's luggage had been carried out of the house, a typed letter, in English, from Mrs. Gandhi, with corrections in her handwriting, was given to Maneka. Its text has never been made public. Observers said that Mrs. Gandhi thought better of the letter and that Maneka chose to suppress it. Maneka sat down and wrote out a reply, in English. Its text somehow found its way into all the national dailies the next morning:

DEAR MUMMY,

As usual you have written a letter meant for posterity and the press. In that are several statements that are, quite simply, not true. The first offense that you keep talking about is "bad language" [apparently, Mrs. Gandhi had accused Maneka of using profanity] and you can produce the family or your people as witnesses but it simply isn't true. Secondly you have talked about Sanjay complaining [about Maneka] when you know, and so does everyone else, of how much affection he had for me.

Now we come to actuals. The indignities and physical and mental abuse I have suffered in the house *no* and I repeat *no* human being would have suffered. As soon as Sanjay died you started literally torturing me in every conceivable way. I have borne it for a long time because of Sanjay and because I am your bahu [daughter-in-law]. If I had wanted to be against you I would not have fought so bitterly for you in the Janata years-—a fact you seem to have conveniently forgotten—when the rest of your family was packed and ready to go abroad. [It was generally thought in New Delhi that this charge applied to Rajiv and Sonia.] I repeat what I have said earlier—I am not political and have no wish to be, but please let me live my life decently without shouting and abusing me all the time. Today you have ordered me to leave this house in front of two witnesses, insulted me in front of the servants, ordered my luggage searched, confiscated my son and told me I cannot take him, abused me in public, called my family names and sacked my servants. For what? I went to the convention as a guest. I spoke & will always speak for you—the rest is up to you. No amount of letters to me will help—but a little bit of affection

will. . . . My son will always be your grandson first and even if
you don't see me, he will come to see you.

> I remain your
> daughter-in-law
> MANEKA

Without further ado, Maneka got into a car with Varun, an
ayah, and a family friend, and with a few belongings, and left the
Prime Minister's house, waving at the reporters and photographers
gathered at the gate. They jumped into their cars and sped after her.
As if to underscore her independence, she went not to her mother's
house but to a little hotel in a fashionable district called the Golf
Links.

Back at the Prime Minister's house, Sharada Prasad, the Prime
Minister's press adviser, telephoned United News of India, a press
agency, and summarized what Mrs. Gandhi had said in that evening's letter to Maneka. His summary, like Maneka's letter, appeared in all the national dailies the next morning:

> Sources close to the Prime Minister said that the differ-
> ences between Mrs. Gandhi and her daughter-in-law arose
> when the latter entered into a secret deal with the R.S.S. leader,
> Sardar Angre, for the sale of the *Surya* magazine. Mrs. Maneka
> Gandhi reportedly did not breathe a word of this to Mrs.
> Gandhi, who felt that the step constituted a total betrayal of all
> the ideals and values Sanjay Gandhi had stood for. Her subse-
> quent actions were all designed to bolster up elements and
> forces hostile to Sanjay Gandhi and to the Prime Minister.
>
> The sources said that although Mrs. Maneka Gandhi had a
> different family background, Mrs. Gandhi and other members
> of the household had accepted her without any reservations as a
> life-partner of Sanjay Gandhi.

Maneka's grandparents on her mother's side were Sikhs, and
many Sikhs were offended by the remark that Mrs. Gandhi, accord-

ing to "sources close to the Prime Minister," made about Maneka's "different family background," even though the same sources had quickly issued several clarifications, saying that there had been no intention of casting aspersions on the Sikhs.

Prasad's summary continues:

> Mrs. Gandhi had also given her unbounded affection and love, the sources said. On many occasions both during Sanjay's life time and later Maneka's actions had been irksome to the family.
>
> However, Mrs. Gandhi always took a lenient view and did nothing except "reproach her gently."
>
> The sources said that Mrs. Maneka Gandhi's latest action in attending the convention in the full knowledge that she [Mrs. Gandhi] was opposed to this meeting was the last straw.
>
> While declaring her faith in Mrs. Gandhi's national leadership and appealing to the people to strengthen her hands, Mrs. Maneka Gandhi in her Lucknow speech had controverted point-by-point all the observations made by the Prime Minister at her impromptu press conference on the previous day.
>
> Mrs. Gandhi had dubbed the convention "anti-party," and as having been encouraged by the R.S.S., the B.J.P. and other elements opposed to her particularly, but Mrs. Maneka Gandhi had blandly denied any link with the R.S.S. . . .
>
> According to sources close to the Prime Minister, there was no question that despite her declaration of faith in Mrs. Gandhi's political leadership, Mrs. Maneka Gandhi was trying to chalk out her own independent political path in alliance with elements which were totally inimical to the Prime Minister and her party. . . .
>
> It is known that immediately after Sanjay's death, Mrs. Maneka Gandhi was sought to be projected in the political field, some writers having even described her as "a real Durga" [warrior goddess: an appellation commonly used for Mrs. Gandhi] who could don the mantle of successor to Mrs. Gandhi better than "mild mannered" Mr. Rajiv Gandhi. Mrs. Maneka Gandhi's mother had also reportedly encouraged these attempts.

In addition, there were some unofficial disclosures of the supposed contents of Mrs. Gandhi's letter, as in this press report:

> Mrs. Gandhi said in her letter that Mrs. Maneka Gandhi
> . . . had consistently been disrespectful towards her even to the
> consternation of Sanjay Gandhi. In their many years of close
> association, Mrs. Gandhi claimed, she had spoken sharply to
> Mrs. Maneka Gandhi only on three occasions: shortly after her
> wedding when she used "vile abuse" against her husband and
> his mother, when Mrs. Maneka Gandhi came to talk about the
> Lucknow convention before Mrs. Gandhi emplaned for London, and on Monday night [March 29th], more "in sorrow than
> in anger."

Maneka called a press conference and tried to counter some of these charges. "There is no question of three occasions," she said. "It is a continuous process." She was particularly scornful of the reference to her "different family background": "I find it ridiculous that [in] this age people can talk about backgrounds and classes. I have always treated human beings as human beings." The following is a newspaper account of some of her other remarks:

> Asked whether she would go back to her mother's house,
> Maneka replied that after marriage no Indian girl goes back to
> her mother. "I will somehow adjust myself independently if
> my mother-in-law does not take me back." She then added: "I
> don't know how I will start a house. I don't have utensils or a
> fridge. I have a take-home salary of Rs 2,317.50 per month."
> [She was the managing director of the Rajdhani General
> Traders, a trucking company started for her by Sanjay.]
> When asked whether she plans to remarry, the 25-year-old
> widow replied: "There are no plans for remarrying again. I am a
> Gandhi." Mrs. Maneka Gandhi said that she was more loyal to
> her mother-in-law than "even to my mother." "Whatever she
> [Mrs. Gandhi] does in her house is her right as mother-in-law."

But she complained to a reporter from the *Indian Express,* in a separate interview, "Ever since Sanjay died, my mail has been censored, my telephone tapped. I had to return all my jewelry and after I came back from Lucknow, I was told not to eat at the family dining table. Their purpose is to isolate me because of some imaginary fears. . . . I feel it is alien to Indian culture to first kick your daughter-in-law out and then write an invective against her and release it to the press. I am very hurt."

There is no issue that is more profound and has greater ramifications in the life of an Indian woman than the fact that she is unable to get married unless her parents can provide her with sufficient dowry. Once she has been given in marriage, she belongs, like her dowry, to her husband's family—to the point where she has practically no rights. The subservient place of a woman in her husband's family has been so notorious that Mrs. Gandhi and her advisers, for all their efforts, were unable to put the row in the Prime Minister's house politically behind them.

After Maneka's expulsion, newspapers started regularly carrying reports of "dowry deaths": the self-immolation of women by fire (until the British banned suttee, in the nineteenth century, some Hindu widows burned themselves on their husbands' funeral pyres), or the murder of women by their husbands, often also by fire, while the women were cooking—deaths that it is notoriously hard to prove are crimes. The "dowry deaths" were a result sometimes of a husband's dissatisfaction with the size of the dowry and sometimes of a husband's wish for a second wife and a second dowry. Whatever a husband's motive, in Hindu society a woman does not have much of a future outside marriage, and a wife may kill herself or allow herself to be killed in preference to enduring the disgrace of being found wanting in her new home. (Among Muslims, a kind of dowry system is not unknown, but it is not standard; a Muslim can have four wives but not four dowries.) The custom of expecting a dowry probably had its origin in Hindu law, which for centuries did not permit the bequest of property to women. The dowry (jewelry, clothes, bedsteads, stools, utensils, even lavish wedding feasts and wedding entertainment) in time became an institutionalized demand by the bridegroom and his parents—a means of obtaining wife support or financial security, or just of supplementing inadequate income. The government passed a Dowry Prohibition Act in 1961, but, like the laws against the caste system and Untouchability, it could not be enforced. (Between 1961 and 1982, there were apparently only eleven prosecutions under it.) The newspapers, for their part, ignored the dowry phenomenon for years; it was simply accepted as one more aspect of crushing Indian poverty, about which little could be done. For months after the row in the Prime Minister's house, however, there was scarcely a day without a newspaper report of at least one "dowry death"— sometimes a dozen such deaths were reported—and a police investigation; and the reports were routinely accompanied by gruesome photographs, interviews with neighbors, reflections by social workers and policemen, and outraged editorials on avaricious, dowry-hungry bridegrooms and in-laws. The *Times of India,* an English-language national daily, declared in August, 1982, "Never before in Indian history has the demand for dowry been so insistent and so widespread and the dowries demanded so large as today." One explanation advanced for the newspapers' newfound interest in the problem was that they were using "dowry death" as a code phrase for Mrs. Gandhi's mistreatment of Maneka, and so were putting the mother-in-law's banishment of the daughter-in-law in the worst possible light.

Once out of the Prime Minister's house, Maneka settled into her hotel in the Golf Links and occupied herself partly with supervising the construction of a veterinary hospital in New Delhi (funded with money that had been mysteriously left to Sanjay by Ruth Cowell, an Australian woman) but mostly with her trucking business. Sanjay, a car enthusiast, had set her up in the business in 1978 by obtaining a loan of two million four hundred thousand rupees from the Oriental Bank of Commerce of Delhi. With the money, he had bought her twenty-two trucks and helped her lease them to the Pure Drinks Company, which was owned by a Congress Indira member of Parliament, and which had been rapidly expanding its market for a soft drink called Campa Cola since 1977, when the Coca-Cola Company pulled out of India rather than observe a new regulation giving the government access to Coca-Cola's proprietary information, including its secret formula. Pure Drinks had paid Maneka a hundred and thirty-two thousand rupees a month for its lease. She had used the money to retire the bank loan and pay herself a salary. But after Maneka was expelled from the Prime Minister's house Pure Drinks suspended the payments, claiming that she owed the company eight hundred thousand rupees for some shelves that it had installed in the drivers' cabins of her trucks. Maneka went to court and got a judgment against the company, and it resumed the payments.

In time, Maneka began touring various states for the Sanjay Five-Point Forum. Wherever she went, she invoked the memory of Sanjay and—sometimes subtly and sometimes not so subtly—appealed to Congress Indira legislators to join her. She had little difficulty getting financial backing from industrial and political malcontents, and little difficulty drawing upon public sympathy, because Mrs. Gandhi was seen by many as having violated one of the major taboos of Indian family life by expelling her widowed daughter-in-law. For the most part, however, Maneka's speeches fell on deaf political ears. Few legislators were prepared to desert Congress Indira—and the power and patronage that went with it at the center and in the states—for a political upstart, and those who did were reviled and were expelled from the Party. Still, operatives from the central government's Intelligence Bureau were said to have been assigned to monitor Maneka's activities and Dumpy's.

Everywhere, the press noted resemblances between Mrs. Gandhi and Maneka: like Mrs. Gandhi, Maneka walked with a quick stride; like Mrs. Gandhi, she went from meeting to meeting repeating simple generalities ("It is not a question of Maneka but of the nation," "We have gathered here not to break a party but to build a nation") and making vague charges ("Leaders are spreading communal tensions," "Weaker sections of society are being hurt," "Anti-social elements are abroad," "Corruption is rooted in the system"). The newspapers used the same term—"schoolgirlish"—to dismiss her speeches that they had used to dismiss Mrs. Gandhi's when she was starting her political career. One day, the newspapers reported that Mrs. Gandhi would be going to the ashram of a holy man (the late Vinoba Bhave) to seek his blessing. On the same day, they reported that Maneka would be going to the same holy man. One day, the youth wing of Congress Indira announced that it would not invite Maneka to any of the functions it was organizing to mark the second anniversary of Sanjay's death. Another day, Maneka and her supporters announced that they would mark that anniversary by calling rallies of widows and distributing clothes to them. (On the anniversary itself, Maneka went with Varun to Sanjay's cremation ground, and an hour later Mrs. Gandhi went there with Rajiv and Sonia and their children.) Maneka's supporters referred to her as "Madam," just as Mrs. Gandhi's supporters referred to *her* as "Madam"—both factions saying things like "Whatever Madam decides, we will abide by it." One Maneka supporter said, "Anybody who is not loyal to Sanjay and his widow cannot be loyal to Rajiv. Anyway, Rajiv is too old. He is thirty-nine. What the country needs is a youth leader, somebody like Madam."

On August 25th, at a press conference, Maneka declared that a lot of members of Congress Indira were becoming dissatisfied with "the nonfunctioning of the government"—it was a phrase that Mrs. Gandhi had used against the Janata government—and that therefore the apolitical Sanjay Forum had to be changed into a political party. "All power is centralized in one house in a group of three or four people," she said. Besides, she contended, workers for the Forum were being harassed, and the only way left was to fight this injustice politically.

The *Times of India* noted in an editorial:

> So finally Mrs. Maneka Gandhi has put her cards on the table. . . . This should put an end to the sedulously propagated myth that she has had no political ambitions, that, apart from her love for animals, her main desire has been to propagate the ideals of her late husband, and that her clash with Mrs. Indira Gandhi leading to her exit from the Prime Minister's house fell in the usual mother-in-law–daughter-in-law category. Indeed, her statement on [August 25th] establishes beyond reasonable doubt that the formation of the [Sanjay Five-Point Forum] earlier this year was a deliberate political act, that Maneka's decision to address its first convention in Lucknow on March 28 amounted to raising the banner of revolt against Mrs. Gandhi. . . .
>
> Maneka has also dropped the pretence that she has no quarrel with Mrs. Gandhi's leadership of the government and the Congress [Indira]. In fact, she has made it clear that the Prime Minister is to be the principal target of her political activities. . . . The fight is thus in the open, which is as well. A political battle, even if it is the result of nothing grander or nobler than a clash of ambitions or personalities, should be fought as a political battle.

The battle was seen as being fought over nothing less than the fate of a nation that was, the national biweekly publication *India Today* said, "a democratic monarchy," and, the publication declared, at stake was the ancestral property—India—with the heir in dispute.

In March, 1983, Maneka formally named her party Rashtriya Sanjay Manch (the National Sanjay Organization), claiming that by then it had established local branches in most states, with a total membership of eight hundred thousand, and asserting that she would take on Rajiv in Amethi in the next general election. Few political observers, though, ever gave Maneka or her emerging party much of a chance, and at the outset it got caught in the crossfire between opposition leaders, who had no use for Sanjay, and Sanjay enthusiasts in Congress Indira, who preferred Mrs. Gandhi and the substance of power to Maneka and the remote possibility of power. Then, in September, three of Maneka's closest supporters, including Dumpy, were arrested, on a charge of murdering a servant. The case was immediately thrown out by the court, and the whole episode, which received much attention in the press, left the impression that Mrs. Gandhi's supporters were bent on destroying Maneka's fledgling organization by any available means—just as Maneka said. The press intensified its attacks on Mrs. Gandhi: on her "cabal"; on her "monolithic, intolerant party"; on her "rule of the states through satraps," chosen more for their loyalty to her than for their popularity in the states; on her "personalized dictatorship." It was pointed out that Mrs. Gandhi was sixty-five, and that Rajiv and the Rajiv men were failing to take hold anywhere. Mrs. Gandhi's supporters continued to dismiss Maneka and the public criticism as a tempest in a teapot. They took comfort in President Reagan's view of Nehru and his descendants. In proposing a toast to Mrs. Gandhi at the White House during her visit to the United States in July, 1982, he had said, "The contributions which your family has made to India most closely parallel in our history the Adams family. They came from Massachusetts, not Kashmir. . . . By coincidence they were often referred to as Boston Brahmins. And theirs, too, was a tradition of scholarship, sacrifice, and public service. Successive generations of Adamses contributed to our national development, first by struggling for independence and articulating our national ideals, then through years of selfless effort toward their attainment. So you, Madam Prime Minister, your father, and each of your sons have served India." The tribute was especially noteworthy since it was paid by a right-wing Republican President to the two Prime Ministers known the world over for their uncompromising Socialist policies.

Early in December, 1982, Mrs. Gandhi surprised everyone by calling elections in January, 1983, for the legislatures of the adjoining southern states of Andhra Pradesh and Karnataka. As a rule, general elections are held every five years, but if at any time the party in power in a state—or in the country—either is forced out of office or voluntarily resigns, and no one else can form a government, special elections may be called. Andhra Pradesh and Karnataka were under Congress Indira rule as it was, but Mrs. Gandhi got the governments there to resign, so that they might return with greater strength. The area had been solidly in Mrs. Gandhi's and her father's camp since Independence, in 1947; and in 1980 she herself had chosen to stand for Parliament from an Andhra Pradesh constituency and had gained a big victory. It was generally assumed, therefore, that the two states would return her party with an overwhelming majority, and so would give her a vote of confidence—something she needed in order to quash Maneka's nascent political career, to consolidate Rajiv's position as the new heir, to offset almost certain defeat in the little northeastern state of Tripura (leftists were in control there, and elections were already scheduled there for January), and to restore some kind of political order to the two states. (The Andhra Pradesh branch of Congress Indira was so faction-ridden that in the course of two years the government there had gone through four chief ministers, and the administration of Karnataka was so corrupt that its chief minister, Gundu Rao, was popularly called Goonda, or Thug.) Above all, she wanted to bolster her own fortunes and those of her party, which were precipitously in decline because of the worsening drought in the country.

In the elections, Congress Indira enjoyed all the advantages.

The campaign period was short, and the opposition was weak and ill-prepared. In Andhra Pradesh, it consisted of the barely nine-month-old regional Telugu Nation Party (Telugu is one of the main South Indian languages), and in Karnataka of disparate regional and national groups, primarily the Janata Party and a party called Kranti Ranga, which was led by a Congress Indira dissident. Top leaders of Mrs. Gandhi's government flew in from New Delhi to campaign, and Mrs. Gandhi and Rajiv themselves crisscrossed hundreds of constituencies, addressing thousands of meetings and reminding everyone that theirs alone was the national party, that they alone were the champions of minorities (Muslims and Untouchables formed sizable populations in both states), and that theirs was the hand that fed the people. (A hand is a Congress Indira symbol.) Meanwhile, Mohammed Yunus, a lifelong friend of the family, published a book he had written about Sanjay, entitled "Son of India," which attacked Maneka's character and asked questions like, as *India Today* put it, "Did Maneka Gandhi remark after her husband, the late Sanjay Gandhi, had been sent to prison: 'There is so much peace with this bastard in jail'? . . . Did she ill-treat Sanjay, driving him to bouts of depression and a risky sport like aerobatics? . . . Did she indulge in wanton revelry after his death, throwing lavish parties and going in fancy dress?" The book was serialized in the *National Herald,* a Congress Indira organ, of which Mrs. Gandhi was a trustee. It was to be released on December 14, 1982, at an official function at the President's house marking the thirty-sixth anniversary of Sanjay's birth, but there was such an outcry in New Delhi against the book, even by Maneka's detractors, that Mrs. Gandhi attended the function but did not say anything about the book, though there were copies of it all over the room. Maneka, for her part, campaigned vigorously in the two states. Throngs greeted her wherever she went. (Rajiv generally got a lukewarm reception.)

Although the opposition had practically no time to muster its forces, the leader of the Telugu Nation Party, Nandamuri Taraka Rama Rao, proved to be a formidable campaigner. He attacked

Mrs. Gandhi and her party for rule of the states through party henchmen, and for corrupt practices, for food shortages, and for inept economic policies. Rao, at fifty-nine, was the most famous Telugu film star. He had acted in some three hundred Telugu films, mostly playing Hindu gods or honest poor men, and he was so closely identified with such roles that some people actually worshipped him as an incarnation of a god come to restore moral order to the country. (In South India, actors in the vernacular cinema are often seen as heroes and are much preferred to venal politicians. The chief minister of the southern state of Tamil Nadu was the most famous Tamil film star, M. G. Ramachandran.) Moreover, many of the opposition candidates, especially in Andhra Pradesh, were better educated and more conversant with local conditions than the Congress Indira candidates.

In perhaps the greatest political upset since Mrs. Gandhi's defeat in 1977, following her hated Emergency, Congress Indira was roundly trounced in both Andhra Pradesh and Karnataka. (It also lost in Tripura.) Maneka's new party had been allotted five places by the Telugu Nation, an alliance of small regional parties, and it won four of them. In due course, the Telugu Nation ministry and the Janata ministry were sworn in in their states.

Political commentators in New Delhi interpreted the election results not only as a defeat for Rajiv and a victory for Maneka but also as a warning that Mrs. Gandhi's own political future and that of her party might be in jeopardy. They pointed out that since Mrs. Gandhi returned to power there had been five other state elections and in none of them had Congress Indira been able to win an absolute majority, and that the strategically important states of Tamil Nadu and West Bengal were under the control of opposition parties. After the loss of Andhra Pradesh and Karnataka, Mrs. Gandhi tried to make a show of strength. She dropped or shuffled members of her Cabinet and the Party high command, and made Rajiv a general secretary, like Sanjay before him. Although the changes were thought to be more cosmetic than substantive, they did help Congress Indira to win a sizable majority in the Delhi municipal elections in February, and so saved her the embarrassment of having the capital under the rule of the opposition.

On November 19, 1982, Mrs. Gandhi opened the Ninth Asian Games, in New Delhi. (At the time, the term "Asian" was elastic in India, and included Middle Eastern, or "West Asian," countries but, in concession to Arab sentiments, not Israel.) They were a Third World version of the Olympics, with five thousand athletes, from thirty-three countries, battling for five hundred and eighty-eight gold, silver, and bronze medals in archery, athletics (or track-and-field sports), badminton, basketball, boxing, cycling, equestrian events, football, golf, gymnastics, handball, hockey, rowing, shooting, swimming, table tennis, tennis, volleyball, weight lifting, wrestling, and yachting. The Games were spoken of in New Delhi as "the most ambitious project India has undertaken in recent years," "the biggest event of the decade," and "the showpiece of the century." *India Today* wrote, "Asiad '82 is India's big bid for international stardom. For 15 days, New Delhi will be making international headlines, for an event that, in terms of prestige, is the biggest stakes India has played for in a long time." In preparation for the Games, New Delhi was for twenty months in the throes of some of the most intensive building activity in memory. Under construction were six gigantic stadiums; a whole new Asian Games Village, with living quarters for five thousand people; three government five-star hotels; nine private five-star hotels; and seven six-lane flyovers, or overpasses. In addition, seven old stadiums and two old hotels were renovated and upgraded; thirty main roads were widened; and a thirty-five-kilometre "ring railway" circling the city was made ready. Television transmitters were modified to broadcast the Games in color in India and also, via satellite, abroad. No expense was spared in landscaping the grounds of the stadiums or in outfitting the stadiums and the hotels with the most up-to-date equipment, which was imported from all parts of the world, at a considerable sacrifice of much-needed foreign exchange. Throughout the preparations, newspapers and magazines were awash with statistics concerning all the construction, gadgetry, and manpower being mobilized: eighty million bricks; a hundred thousand tons of cement; ninety thousand tons of steel; five hundred thousand flowering plants and bushes; three hundred kilometres of cables and wires; twelve thousand telephone lines; a hundred and twenty-five thousand laborers brought in from other parts of the country; two thousand six hundred technical officials; two thousand general officials; six hundred liaison officials and receptionists; two thousand men from the Indian Army and the Border Security Force; and a thousand ushers. In the words of a newspaper article written shortly before the Games, "Delhi is in much the same state as a bride is before her wedding."

The Games went back to the time of Prime Minister Jawaharlal Nehru, who in 1951, in New Delhi, presided over the First Asian Games, in which nearly five hundred athletes, from eleven countries, took part. The Games had since been held every four years or so, in Manila, Tokyo, Jakarta, and Bangkok, among other places, the participants sometimes including Iran, Iraq, and Kuwait. Mr. Nehru's daughter's government named the biggest of the new stadiums the Jawaharlal Nehru Stadium. Its grounds occupied more than ninety acres in the heart of the city. It had a seating capacity of seventy-five thousand. Looming above the stadium were four cantilevered steel towers with the scores of fluorescent lights required for the floodlighting of the sports events and for television transmission in color. The lights were kept on all night long, and the glow was visible from almost every part of the city, as if to remind people of the incongruity of the new stadiums amid Mogul monuments and ruins. Rajiv's first main task as a politician was to oversee the construction of the stadiums; Mrs. Gandhi apparently chose her sixty-fifth birthday to inaugurate the Games; and the "glamour events" of the Games were held in the Jawaharlal

Nehru Stadium. The stadiums were soon being referred to in New Delhi as memorials in brick and mortar—as it were, latter-day Pyramids—to the Nehru-Gandhi family.

The cost of constructing all these facilities ballooned after 1976, which was when the Asian Games Federation decided to hold the Ninth Games in India. At that time, the cost was estimated at six hundred million rupees. Then, before any preparations could get under way, Mrs. Gandhi was thrown out of office. Prime Minister Morarji Desai's Janata government, in office from 1977 to 1979, did nothing about the Games, because it was preoccupied with other matters, and Prime Minister Charan Singh's splinter-Janata caretaker government—which was in office for only a few months, during the campaign for the general election of 1980, in which Mrs. Gandhi made a triumphant return to power—was so shaky that it did nothing about anything. Anyway, Charan Singh called the Games a "costly tamasha" and said he was considering reneging on India's commitment. When Mrs. Gandhi returned to office, in January, 1980, it was resolved immediately, in her first Cabinet meeting, that the government should forge ahead with the preparations. But there were further delays, as a result of changes in her Cabinet and in a Special Organizing Committee set up for the Games. Thereafter, the buildings went up with such speed that a local architect remarked in wonder, "It's a miracle. It's as if dogs suddenly started walking on two legs." Because everything had to be built quickly, the work of construction went on around the clock, laborers working day shifts and night shifts, and the frenetic pace, which created conditions for hoarding and black-marketeering, added enormously to the cost. At one time, there were at least twenty-eight committees working on the Games, most of them filled with Congress Indira members and civil servants, and none of them having a sports figure for chairman or vice-chairman. Huge sums of money were made illegally by politicians in power, who had the exclusive authority to grant licenses, and by contractors, who had never had so much work before. The respected South Indian newspaper *Hindu* reported:

The whole exercise is being transformed by unscrupulous entrepreneurs with political pull into a money spinning operation.

It has led to widespread hoarding and black-marketing of construction material pushing up the costs and, in the process, filling the pockets of the privileged few who are able to make a big kill in the name of keeping to the deadline. . . .

Big hoteliers and traders have used every big international conference held in Delhi during the last two decades to push up prices. . . . After the Asian Games, [the price of a hotel room] will be increased to over Rs. 1,000 a day with the excuse that construction, renovation and maintenance costs have shot up.

Most Indians did not earn a thousand rupees in six months.

In the sixth five-year plan, instituted in 1980, the total expenditure allocated for sports, youth programs, and welfare was a hundred and seventy million rupees, of which a hundred million was supposed to go for sports. But the official estimates for the construction and other activities associated with the Ninth Asian Games ran to three billion six hundred million rupees, and unofficial estimates ran anywhere from six billion to ten billion. It was said that if what was spent on the Asian Games had been invested in, for instance, village and other small industries it would have resulted in permanent employment for at least two million people. (The total investment in village and other small industries for the fiscal year 1981–82 was put at two billion seven hundred million rupees, while receipts for the total budget of the Indian government for the fiscal year 1981–82 were estimated at a hundred and forty billion rupees, and expenditures at a hundred and fifty billion.)

A few weeks before the Games began, I visited the nearly completed Indraprastha Indoor Stadium, which was billed as the third-largest domed stadium in the world. (Only the ones in Houston and New Orleans were bigger.) It occupied a hundred-and-ten-acre site on the right bank of the sacred Yamuna River, by a temple in honor of Hanuman, the monkey god, and Shiva, Rama, and Sita. Below the dome, of shimmering aluminum, it had what looked like portholes all around; in fact, it might have been a gigantic flying saucer. The stadium site was surrounded by barbed wire, like a concentration camp, and inside were thousands of laborers racing to finish the work—wasted, half-clad men, women, and children covered with dust, many of them high up on scaffolding and weighted down with head loads. On swampy ground surrounding the structure were still more thousands of laborers, cooking, washing, sleeping—whole families living under a piece of canvas or bamboo matting held up by a couple of sticks. A lucky few huddled under plastic sheets. Such slums are a standard sight in New Delhi: they dot every cranny in the city—under the new flyovers, behind houses, beside monuments. But around the stadium and at its gates were security guards, trying to bar access to anyone seeking out the laborers and, as far as possible, to keep them hidden from view.

I came armed with the necessary government permission and, after much screening, was allowed to talk to a few of the laborers. They were voluble in their complaints. They said that they couldn't find drinking water, that they didn't have food, that there were no latrines. They said that they knew neither the language nor the laws of New Delhi—most of them were from South India, and I had to use an interpreter—and that they had been picked up by recruiting agents of the contractor and brought to New Delhi in truckloads. They said that the recruiting agents had got them to put their thumbprints on a piece of paper, and had told them that that was a guarantee of high wages, but that in New Delhi they were being paid only eleven rupees a day and had no idea where the paper was or where the recruiting agents were. They said they were afraid that as soon as the work on the project was finished their hutments would be bulldozed and they would be trucked penniless to who knew what destination.

An official joined me and overheard some of their complaints. "All societies have been industrialized by the sweat of the poor," he said to me over their heads. "The weakest have to go to the wall or we'll all be sunk. In a country of cannibals, if one isn't a cannibal one will perish." He added guiltily, "God help us."

Newspapers pointed out that the new buildings added to the shortages of electricity, drinking water, and land in the city. They said that the buildings required between fifty and seventy-five additional megawatts of electricity per day, whereas the previous average daily power consumption for New Delhi had been about five hundred and fifty megawatts. And for years there had been frequent power cuts, with the newspapers daily publishing notices like this one, from the *Times of India*: "Because of general repairs, power supply will be affected tomorrow between 9 a.m. and 2 p.m. to C and H Blocks Naraina Vihar, C, F and H Blocks Kirti Nagar residential, part of Manohar Park, Jyoti Colony, Circular Road, Jawala Nagar; and between 9 a.m. and 6 p.m. to part of Amar Colony, Lajpat Nagar-IV and Basant Village." In fact, by all accounts the generating equipment and the distribution system in the city—and in the rest of the country—had long been in considerable disrepair. After the construction got under way, there were, on the average, twelve electrical breakdowns a day in the city. Even without the new buildings, the number of consumers of electricity in New Delhi had doubled in the last five years, and yet the number of skilled workers maintaining and servicing the equipment had not increased. The electricity for the stadiums and the hotels had to come from neighboring states, and this meant creating shortages there. And, in any event, in many parts of the country industrial machinery was already being shut down for lack of electricity.

In New Delhi, the new construction meant that poor people were dispossessed, acres of land needed for hospitals, schools, and inexpensive housing were lost, and some of the best green areas were denuded. One day, a newspaper reported that nine hundred poor families had been displaced; that work had had to be stopped on a ten-story, five-hundred-bed hospital, because of the diversion of building materials; and that about a thousand mature trees had been felled, with a threatened increase in dust pollution. Even enthusiasts of the Games conceded that, given the flow of traffic then, the main roads did not need to be broadened and the flyovers did not need to be built. (The flyovers, however, have since become invaluable, because of a great increase in traffic, brought about by an almost continuous migration of people to the capital.)

The government slogan for the Asian Games was "1982 is the year of sportsmen and sportswomen and the common man." India had never done particularly well at the Games. (The Japanese, the Chinese, and the South Koreans had usually walked away with the most gold medals.) Before the Games, the Indian athletes were given blood tests, and it was discovered that all the women and ten per cent of the men were anemic. As for the government's "common man," he was not able to see the Games. A brisk black market in tickets developed. Businessmen cornered huge blocks of them in order to present them to politicians and officials from whom they wanted favors; a ticket could hardly be had for a hundred rupees. A government brochure said:

> So, come and experience the wonder that is India in the Year of the Asiad . . . with Sport and Tourism happily blending for benefit, and let your talisman be "Appu" [the Game's mascot]—our particularly auspicious baby elephant, who is known for his wisdom, strength, and loyalty and who is already prancing playfully as he impatiently awaits your arrival in this ancient land of Kings, Palaces, Monuments, Festivals, Temples and Tombs. On his forehead he carries the mark of a "Bindiya"—the Symbol of the IX Asian Games. India is a perpetual siren and Delhi will surpass its promise, as it prepares to give you a carnival-mood welcome . . . a sunburst of fun and glory.

But the image of Appu did not become widely known in India; countrywide Appu sports clubs and franchises had been planned, but they didn't catch on with Indians, to say nothing of foreign tourists. "Appu, the prancing elephant, the IX Asiad's mascot, has also become a symbol of the white elephant that many people believe the Games will be as far as the country is concerned," *India Today* wrote before the Games, and on another occasion it quoted a member of the Special Organizing Committee as saying, "There should have been an Asiad fever in the capital. But everyone just seems to be happy because flyovers have opened. Outside Delhi, no one seems to be aware of the big event in November." At the time of the Games, some hotels were only half finished, and tourists and visiting sportsmen and sportswomen had to negotiate scaffoldings to get to and from their rooms. The tourist season in India lasts only from October to March, when the weather is comfortable. At the time, there was talk that when the hotels were finally completed their rooms would be rented out as commercial offices— accommodations for which licenses would never ordinarily be granted, because of the great housing shortage in New Delhi, but for which there is a constant demand, because every state government and major business feels that it needs an office in the capital. "It would be interesting to know why those who had been granted special quotas and extraordinary concessions to get hotel complexes ready in time for the Asian Games failed to deliver the goods," wrote the *Statesman,* a highly respected English-language Indian daily. "The fact that even the available hotel accommodation has not been fully utilized for the Games should not let the guilty get away unpunished." But the newspaper's plea was essentially rhetorical: guilty profiteers routinely get away unpunished, just as newspapers routinely decry them.

The government established a new Sports Ministry, but people were left to wonder what it would eventually do with the stadiums and the Asian Games Village—how their maintenance would be paid for and how they would be used. There were no local sports events or cultural events that could conceivably justify the expense of lighting and air-conditioning the various facilities, and people were afraid that the stadiums would end up being used for political rallies, as happened in Perón's Argentina and Mussolini's Italy. The Asian Games Village had "the largest kitchen" in the country, with deep-freeze and cold-storage capacity for forty tons of food, and it had a dining area capable of feeding two thousand people at a time, and also the biggest cultural center in the country, a reception center, a discothèque, a hundred-and-eighty-four-foot water tower with a viewing gallery at the top, and a couple of hundred duplex apartments with private, enclosed terraces and space for private gardens. The government eventually recovered the cost of some of the apartments by auctioning them off to prosperous Indians living abroad. The other apartments were retained for occasional international competitions. (The government succeeded in enticing the Afro-Asian Games to New Delhi, to be held in 1983, and tried, unsuccessfully, to lure the 1992 Olympic Games.) Whatever might happen, it was hard to imagine any useful purpose that the public facilities could possibly serve.

The Asian Games were considered to have been a failure. The expected attendance from the country and abroad never materialized. Venders, who had obtained expensive government licenses to supply ice cream, say, complained that they had been stuck with their goods. But the sports events themselves went off without a hitch—a circumstance that the press celebrated exuberantly. "As one spectator was overheard remarking after watching the proceedings for a week: 'If only they could run the country like this, India wouldn't have a care in the world,'" *India Today* wrote. "As a diplomatic and public relations coup, the Games had no rival since Independence." Most of the time, however, the Games seemed to be a contest between the Japanese and the Chinese. Indians won only thirteen gold medals out of a hundred and ninety-six. (Indians were defeated even in field hockey, which, with cricket, is one of the two most popular sports in India, and the defeat was especially galling because it was inflicted by the Pakistanis.) But people tried to put a good face on the outcome. One columnist wrote, "If all these fancy athletes from abroad are really such hot shots, let them stay in Delhi for a decent interval, drink the water we drink, eat the food we eat, socialize with the mosquitoes we socialize with, and then compete with us."

Rajiv Gandhi and Rama's Kingdom

In 1983, in addition to the row between Maneka and Mrs. Gandhi, and the complications created by the Games and their facilities, people were exercised about caste wars (in some parts of the country, Brahmans had razed entire villages of Untouchables); about spreading banditry in the countryside (in June, the chief minister of Uttar Pradesh had resigned because he was not able to control banditry in his state); about a precipitous rise in malaria (bad sanitation everywhere was breeding mosquitoes, and the mosquitoes had become insecticide-resistant); about a virulent outbreak of dengue fever (half of New Delhi was down with it in one season); about the government's increasing reliance on the Army to maintain law and order (in two states, in the summer of 1982, mutinous police indulged in mob violence, and order was restored only when the Army was called in); about the economic "boomlet" in the country (since returning to power, Mrs. Gandhi had gradually relaxed some of the socialist controls in order to encourage capitalist-type investments, and the consequent perpetual shortages and black-marketeering had put up the price of everything); about Mrs. Gandhi's growing international lustre (in 1982, she had visited England, America, and the Soviet Union, to great public acclaim in each country, and in March of 1983 she had taken over from Fidel Castro the chairmanship of a conference of nonaligned nations that was held in New Delhi); about her diplomatic coup in obtaining enriched uranium (apparently, the French, with the approval of the Reagan Administration, would, after all, supply fuel for the Tarapur nuclear plant, near Bombay, without all the safeguards that the American government had previously insisted on); about dangers to Indian security from Afghanistan (ever since the time of Mahmud of Ghazni, who lived from 971 to 1030, Hindu India had been overrun by armies of Muslim invaders coming from Central Asia through the region of Afghanistan and the Khyber Pass); about various attempts to silence the press (the state of Bihar almost passed an Emergency-type press-censorship bill, which was regarded as a trial balloon for a similar national bill); and about the opening of the film "Gandhi," which had aroused feelings of national pride not known since the early years of Independence. (The government had helped finance the British film, over protests by the Indian film industry, and its success around the world was seen as Mrs. Gandhi's greatest propaganda coup.) Beneath all these concerns—and expressed in discussions of India's purchase of four million tons of wheat from America, of the blighted weather in 1982, and of the government's ineptitude in giving emergency aid to farmers—moved the spectre of famine, for the land was in the grip of what seemed to be the worst drought of the century, and some hundred million people were reported to be on the verge of starvation; in fact, the drought at the time in West Bengal and Bihar had revived memories of the Great Bengal Famine of 1943, in which as many as three million people may have died. Food in the stomach seemed, as always, to be the main preoccupation of the people of India.

2

The Turban
and the Cap

A demand by the Sikhs for some kind of special status had been ticking like a bomb in the background almost since the Partition. In a sense, the Sikhs' quest for political power in independent India had its roots in the Muslim quest for political power in British India which in 1947 resulted in the Partition and the creation of Pakistan. It was at that time that some Sikhs first raised the cry for Khalistan (the name means "a pure place for Sikhs"), as if to say that, since the Muslims had got Pakistan ("a pure place for Muslims"), the Sikhs deserved no less. But most people, including the Sikh community as a whole, treated the cry only as a protest against the Partition and the accompanying riots, which left tens of thousands of Sikhs dead and many times that number refugees—a fate that they shared, of course, with Hindus and Muslims. After all, Muslims in pre-Partition India numbered in the tens of millions, and Islam was a recognized world religion, whereas Sikhs were members of a much smaller minority, of only a few million, and Sikhism had for centuries been regarded as a "sect" of Hinduism. Sikhs, however, had always enjoyed political influence out of proportion to their number, perhaps because they were a fierce, mercurial, and volatile minority united by their language and by a strict monotheistic religion. Born out of strife and anarchy in the fifteenth century, Sikhism soon became famous for its warlike traditions and rigid religious practices. Then the Sikh guru Gobind Singh (1666–1708) initiated five of his disciples, from different Hindu castes, into a casteless martial brotherhood called the Khalsa ("the pure") by having them drink nectar from the same bowl, stirred with a double-edged dagger, and by giving them a new surname, Singh, which means "lion." He had each of the lions vow never to cut his hair or his beard and always to wear a comb in his hair, a steel bracelet, a sabre at his side, and knee-length drawers. These external symbols of faith immediately identified each lion as a member of the Khalsa, just as the wearing of a military uniform might have. Many Sikh theologians think that Gobind Singh intended the Khalsa to be an army of soldier-saints, a sort of militant theocracy, and, in fact, many Sikhs came to refer to their brotherhood as "the army." The guru, proclaiming all Sikhs equal, asked to be received into the Khalsa himself, and after this was done he declared that the succession of Sikh gurus was at an end, and that the Granth—a compendium of the teachings, sayings, and hymns of various Sikh gurus (and of Hindu and Muslim saints as well), selected and completed in 1604 by Arjun, the fifth of the ten gurus of the Sikhs—was thereafter to be the personal, immortal guru of every Sikh. Within a few days, eighty thousand followers and disciples of Gobind Singh had joined the Khalsa. Most Sikhs eventually became members of it and, despite the hot climate and the exigencies of modern life, continued to wear the symbols of their faith.

In 1956, the Indian government, trying to deal with chauvinist linguistic minorities, divided up some states to create new ones for some of the major linguistic groups. But no state was created for the Sikhs, because their language, Punjabi, was spoken by two or three times as many Hindus. In fact, Nehru dismissed their demand—vociferously pressed—for their own separate state as one patently based on religion rather than on language, and inimical to the principles of a secular country. But the Sikhs in the state of East Punjab (West Punjab had become part of Pakistan) were more interested in their own cause than in that of the country, and in subsequent years they redoubled their agitation. Finally, in 1966, Mrs. Gandhi's government divided East Punjab into two states: Punjab, where Sikhs were predominant, and Haryana, where Hindus were predominant. The two states, however, were forced to share the Union Territory of Chandigarh. Lahore, the capital of the old British province of the Punjab, had gone to Pakistan, and Chandigarh had been built, at great expense, to replace it as a capital city. The Sikhs wanted to have Chandigarh to themselves, because the city, which had been designed in the late nineteen-forties by the French architect Le Corbusier, seemed to hold a certain exotic glamour for them. In addition, they complained that some of the towns and districts given to Haryana should have been awarded to them. They were also unhappy about the formula for sharing the waters of the Ravi and Beas Rivers with Haryana and the neighboring state of Rajasthan: they wanted more of the water for the irrigation of their own state. The government contended that the Sikhs were too few to justify its giving them what they wanted, and that the Sikhs would have ended up being a minority if the new state of Punjab had been awarded more territory, for they had a bare majority there as it was. Then, even after the Sikhs got their state, they were seldom able to form Sikh state governments or to send a bloc of Sikh representatives to the Parliament, in New Delhi, because, it turned out, Sikhs did not automatically vote for candidates of the Akali Dal, the Sikh religious party. Different Sikh caste groups in Punjab had different political interests, depending on what they did and where they lived: the Khatris were business-men in the towns; the Jats were independent farmers in the villages; the Mazhabis were landless laborers with the status of Untouchables. (Although in theory Sikhism does not recognize caste, in practice Sikhs retain the castes of their Hindu ancestors.) According to the last available statistics, the Khatris constituted about ten per cent of the Sikh population in Punjab, the Jats about fifty-five per cent, and the Mazhabis about thirty-five per cent. The Akali Dal could rely only on the support of the Jats, a fiery, orthodox people—they were the backbone of the extremist movement—with the result that it often had to form coalition governments in the state with the Congress Indira or the Jana Sangh.

In 1972, the Akali Dal appointed a committee of Sikhs, representing the many shades of opinion within the Party, to examine the causes of Sikh political failure, and to redefine the Party's policies and program and, by extension, the demands that Sikhs should make of the central government. In October of 1973, this committee presented its report to the Party in the town of Anandpur Sahib, the ancestral home of the guru Gobind Singh; having militarized the faith, he had built a series of fortresses with the town at the center. After some discussion, the report was adopted, and came to be known as the first Anandpur Sahib resolution. None of its demands were satisfied. In 1977, the Party met in the town of Ludhiana and passed another resolution, the second Anandpur Sahib resolution. The two resolutions seemed to overlap. The second repeated and amplified the tenets of the first, but, because the Akali Dal happened to be riding high in 1977, thanks to the Janata Party's defeat of Mrs. Gandhi at the polls after the Emergency, the second resolution was more moderate in tone. Then, in 1980, when the Congress Indira defeated the Janata Party, and Mrs. Gandhi was returned by a big majority, Sikh politics took an extremist turn. The Akali Dal called for immediate implementation of the Anandpur Sahib resolutions, and Sant Jarnail Singh Bhindranwale, a Jat monk, started using terrorist means to get the government to capitulate. At the same time, he appealed to the fundamentalist side of the Sikh faith, and those appeals made it difficult for Sikh moderates to stand up to him. When the government tried to arrest him, he took refuge in the Golden Temple, in Amritsar, and carried on his campaign from there. The temple, which was built in the sixteenth century, is the seat of the oldest surviving copy of the Granth and is the holiest of all Sikh shrines. Mrs. Gandhi followed the same policy with the extremist Sikhs that had proved successful in keeping other restive minorities in check: she put the state under President's Rule—an emergency constitutional provision according to which the central government can temporarily rule a state from New Delhi when it deems that law and order have broken down in the state—and thereupon engaged in a combination of ruthless military suppression and endless political negotiation, calculated to divide her opposition and wear it down.

The Anandpur Sahib resolutions had all along been the touchstone of Sikh politics, but they were written in Punjabi, a minor regional language, and in Gurmukhi, an unfamiliar script, so for years they were scarcely known outside councils of the Akali Dal. Few literate Sikhs had read them, and most unlettered Sikhs knew about them only through slogans and by hearsay. The first English translation was not available until 1981, and it was a bowdlerized and much-shortened version. I can read Punjabi, but I was not able to get hold of the original texts; no one I asked for information had ever set eyes on them. Since 1980, the resolutions had been constantly referred to and invoked in crucial negotiations, but various Sikh leaders had been using various versions, rather than a single authorized text.

There were at least two working versions: an extremist version, issued by the extremist Sikh leader Jagdev Singh Talwandi around 1981, and a so-called authenticated version, issued in 1983 by Sant Harchand Singh Longowal, the temperate president of the Akali Dal. Both denounced the Hindus in Punjab, who supported the Congress Indira or the Jana Sangh. Sometimes both seemed to say that in respect to Punjab the central government should have responsibility only for defense, external affairs, currency, and general communications, and in all other respects Punjab should have complete authority; it was as if the Sikhs were demanding a special kind of relationship with the Indian Union. And sometimes both seemed to say that all states should enjoy the rights they wanted for

Punjab, as if they were asking for a total overhaul of the federal structure and the Indian Constitution. Perhaps because the drafters wanted to avoid treasonous language, and also because the resolutions they hammered out were compromises, the various demands and assertions were vague; neither of the resolutions, for instance, made any direct reference to secession or to Khalistan. But the Talwandi version maintained that "the brute majority in India, in 1950, has imposed a constitutional arrangement on India which denudes the Sikhs of their political identity, and subordinates them as a cultural particularity, thus liquidating the Sikhs politically and exposing them to spiritual death and cultural decay." It demanded that "an autonomous region in the north of India should be set up forthwith wherein the Sikhs' interests are constitutionally recognized as of primary and special importance," adding that "the Sikh autonomous region may be conceded and declared as entitled to frame its own constitution on the basis of having all powers to and from itself except foreign relations, defense, and general communication." Longowal's authenticated version made no reference to "liquidating the Sikhs politically" or to the setting up of an "autonomous region" or to that region's having a right "to frame its own constitution." It called for the creation of a new, expanded Punjab for the Sikhs, which would include not only Chandigarh but all the disputed areas excluded from the state of Punjab, and in which the Akali Dal would extirpate atheism and "un-Sikh thinking" and propagate the Sikh way of life. It also called for the religious and political preëminence of the Khalsa in the new, expanded Punjab, and a "congenial environment and a political setup" to bring it about. The exact words of the various texts are of little consequence. In rallying the Sikh masses, what mattered was the cry "The Anandpur Sahib resolutions!" This was the cry of Bhindranwale, and any Sikh leader who muted this cry was liable to be pushed aside in favor of a leader who was shriller.

The odd thing was that Sikhism not only had long been considered a sect of Hinduism but also, historically, had seemed always to be at war with Islam. Then, in the eighties, the Sikhs began to emphasize their monotheistic beliefs, to say that their religion had less in common with polytheistic Hinduism than with monotheistic Islam, and to agitate for a change in the status of Sikhism in the Constitution from a sect of Hinduism to a religion. Sikh extremists were indulging in excesses like those of the followers of Ayatollah Khomeini in Iran. In the new, fanatical atmosphere of violence and intimidation, civil liberties, which had never had much meaning for the poor, began to have less and less meaning for the well-off, as the Sikh extremists attempted assassinations and resorted to hijacking and rioting to gain public attention to their cause. Over the years, Mrs. Gandhi's government had created states for other ethnic or cultural minorities in order to defuse their movements for autonomy or independence, only to see the movements reappear, sometimes in more virulent forms, much as the Sikhs' had done.

In June, 1982, in a new attempt to mollify the Sikhs, Mrs. Gandhi chose a Sikh named Zail Singh as her party's candidate for President of India. He was just able to speak, read, and write English, the language of the government and the lingua franca of the country. The son of a carpenter turned farmer, he was born, in 1916, in a village in what was then the princely state of Faridkot, which was notorious for its tyrannical rule. He had received a parochial education and had made his name in the regional politics of the Punjab mainly by reciting Sikh scriptures in Sikh temples and by organizing militant protests against the British and the tyranny in Faridkot. He had risen to become the Congress Party chief minister of the new Punjab state in 1972 and had held the office until 1977, but he had remained essentially a regional figure until 1980, when Mrs. Gandhi made him Minister of Home Affairs in her Cabinet. As Home Affairs Minister, he came under considerable public criticism for praising Hitler in Parliament as a great leader. (He continued to contend that Hitler, though mad, did some good. "Remember, it was Hitler's war which ultimately forced Britain to cut its losses abroad and give freedom to India— and to the other colonies," he told an interviewer in the summer of 1982.)

The six Presidents so far had all been national or international figures, and Mrs. Gandhi's selection of Zail Singh was widely derided. The magazine *Organiser* referred to him as a court jester, and the *Indian Express* called him "Caligula's horse"; for some reason, the Roman emperor Caligula, who made his horse a consul, seemed to have caught the Indian reading public's imagination in that year, and the name of Zail Singh was hardly ever mentioned without a reference to the horse. Zail Singh, however, was not without his admirers. They said that he had been a heroic fighter for Indian freedom—more heroic than many better-known leaders, because his struggle had been carried on in Faridkot, where he was subjected to all kinds of primitive tortures. They pointed out that as chief minister of Punjab he had managed to keep Sikh extremists at bay. They maintained that criticism of him stemmed from Indians' hatred of their own rustic nature.

The President of India functions mostly as a figurehead, but there are ambiguities in the constitution about his exact powers. For instance, only the President can proclaim a national emergency—under the constitution, when there is a grave internal or external threat to national security the government can suspend civil liberties under such a proclamation—but the proclamation of an emergency has to be recommended by the Prime Minister and the Cabinet. It was said that Fakhruddin Ali Ahmed, who was the President when Mrs. Gandhi recommended an emergency proclamation, had grave doubts that any threat to national security existed—indeed, felt that Mrs. Gandhi was recommending the proclamation only to shore up her waning power—but, because he had a narrow view of the powers of the President, he deferred to the Prime Minister and proclaimed an emergency. Another President, with a more expansionist view of the President's powers, might have rejected the recommendation and carried the day, since under the constitution the President is also the commander-in-chief of the armed forces.

At the time of Zail Singh's nomination, the opposition, as if to dramatize the Presidential role in proclaiming the 1975 Emergency, settled on H. R. Khanna to stand against him. Khanna had been a judge of the Supreme Court during the Emergency and had sat on a celebrated case in which some Emergency prisoners argued that there were certain "fundamental" civil liberties, like habeas corpus, that could never be suspended under the constitution. The court had sided with the government, but Khanna had dissented. The presumption was, therefore, that Khanna would be a strong, independent President, while Zail Singh would be merely Mrs. Gandhi's stooge. For years, Zail Singh had been known as a "great toady" of the Nehru-Gandhi family. He had called Sanjay his "savior" and now predicted that Rajiv would turn out to be another Jawaharlal Nehru. During the Presidential campaign, he declared, referring to Mrs. Gandhi, "If my leader had said I should pick up a broom and be a sweeper, I would have done that. She chose me to be President." Sweepers are Untouchables, so even in the Indian political context, which abounds in homely similes and outlandish hyperbole, the remark stood out.

The President, who serves a five-year term, is chosen, customarily in July or August, by the elected members of Parliament and of the state legislative assemblies. Since in 1982 these bodies were largely under Congress Indira control, Zail Singh was easily elected. He moved into the President's house—one of the most magnificent buildings in which any Indian ruler has ever lived. Built by the British architect Sir Edwin Lutyens between 1921 and 1929, when New Delhi was being developed as the new capital of imperial India, it served as a home for the viceroys. It has three hundred and forty rooms, including thirty-seven salons, and one and a half miles of corridors. The building alone extends over five acres, and it has grounds of four hundred acres. It and its satellite buildings house Presidential staff members and hangers-on numbering some ten thousand. In fact, it is almost a little township within New

Delhi, with its own school, its own cinemas, and its own swimming pool, tennis court, and golf course. People expressed amazement that a rustic Sikh should have moved into such a palace only a few months after a young widow of Sikh ancestry moved out of the Prime Minister's house.

As it turned out, despite a Sikh President, negotiations between the Sikhs and Mrs. Gandhi's government did not make much headway. In fact, for months the Sikhs resorted to sustained direct-action agitation, in which about a hundred thousand of them were jailed and about a hundred and fifty died, mostly at the hands of the police. The moderate Sikhs in Punjab failed to get anywhere with Mrs. Gandhi, and their failure gave impetus to Bhindranwale's extremist faction: around February, 1983, his followers started a terrorist campaign, shooting and knifing public officials and Hindu villagers, and burning Hindu houses and shops, to force Mrs. Gandhi to yield to Punjab (and to other states) political authority in all areas except defense, foreign relations, communications, railways, and currency. Bhindranwale's extremists gained the ascendancy among the Sikhs, with the result that the once moderate leader Longowal issued a "do or die" declaration in April, 1983, notifying the government that his followers would take the law into their own hands from then on, and sounded a call for an "army" of volunteers prepared to sacrifice their lives for greater political autonomy for the Sikhs. Both the moderate and the extremist Sikhs were only echoing the demands, mutatis mutandis, of other national minorities, like the Nagas, the Mizos, and the Assamese.

Starting in December, 1979, a volatile mass protest movement led by students in the state of Assam practically paralyzed the functioning of the government there. The protesters demanded the disfranchisement or expulsion of all the Bengali migrants who since 1951, attracted by Assam's sparse population and rich resources, had been coming in from the east—from what had been East Pakistan and in 1971 became the nation of Bangladesh, and from the state of West Bengal. By 1983, there were some four million Bengalis in Assam, constituting a fifth of the state's population. They stuck out as a visible foreign presence in Assam's essentially rural landscape, because they congregated in the few cities and in squatter communities. Besides, most of the Bengalis were Muslims, and most of the Assamese were Hindus; and most of the Bengalis were poor refugees, and the Assamese considered them a blight on the Assamese way of life and economic and political power. Mrs. Gandhi had all along rejected the protesters' demands, contending that to give in on the issue of disfranchisement would create different classes of citizens, and that there was no way to repatriate any of the migrants to Bangladesh (because, among other things, Bangladesh denied the existence of any Bangladeshi refugees in Assam) or to deport them to another state (because doing so would only transfer the Bengali problem elsewhere). She contended that the government could not tolerate a challenge to its authority in Assam and hope to make a stand against the demands of other religious, ethnic, and linguistic minorities, such as the Sikhs. (Assam itself had about two million tribal people, who had been agitating for a separate territory, but in the early eighties their agitation was only smoldering.) Over the years, Mrs. Gandhi tried to defuse the Assamese protest movement by dissolving the legislative assembly, by suspending civil liberties, and by taking disciplinary action against government workers who participated in protests; for nearly a year, she held talks with the protest leaders in Delhi. The discussions were having some success, but even the more moderate leaders would not give in on the issue of disfranchisement of at least some of the Bengalis. (The initial Bengali Partition refugees were accorded a higher legal status than, for instance, Bangladeshi refugees, who came twenty years later.) Assamese leaders claimed that Mrs. Gandhi was holding out on the issue only because the Bengalis provided her and her party a bank of automatic votes.

Early in 1983, Mrs. Gandhi precipitated a head-on confrontation with the Assamese protesters. She called an election for Assam's legislative assembly and also for Parliament in February, even though the protesters had said that they would boycott any election in which all the Bengalis were voting. Since March, 1982, her government had ruled Assam under President's Rule. Under the constitution, it could have continued the President's Rule beyond a year by a two-thirds vote of Parliament, but Mrs. Gandhi decided to gamble on the election. The stakes were enormous. The boycott would assure a victory for her and her party and offset in some measure the defeats in the south, but there could be violence that would be difficult to control.

In Assam, the election campaign was carried on almost at gunpoint. At least fifty battalions of paramilitary forces were deployed to maintain order. Parties refrained from announcing their candidates until the last possible moment, for fear of mob reprisals. Fifty per cent of the Congress Indira candidates from Assam were Bengalis and Muslims, and they spoke at rallies only at the risk of their lives. Many of them moved with armed guards. (One Congress Indira candidate for Parliament from Assam was shot dead while he was addressing a political rally.) Bridges, roads, and railway tracks were blown up, fragmenting Assam's population and making orderly polling almost impossible. Although in the election Congress Indira gained a huge majority in the legislative assembly and won all the seats in Parliament, the election was attended by one of the worst outbreaks of Hindu-Muslim violence since the Partition. In Assam, more than five thousand people, most of them Bengalis and many of them women and children, were killed by mobs carrying spears and knives. Perhaps as many as three hundred thousand Bengalis were made refugees, and were soon living in refugee camps in Assam and in neighboring states. During the election campaign, Assam was virtually under military rule.

Mrs. Gandhi, dedicated to preventing the fabric of the federal union from coming unravelled, employed against the Sikhs a policy she had employed, with varying degrees of success, against, for instance, the Assamese: she equivocated; she played off extremists against moderates, using one to discredit the other. Behind her maneuverings, there was always the threat of military action, which in the nineteen-seventies she had used to crush Naga and Mizo rebellions. In fact, between 1980 and 1983 she had actually encouraged a movement of Sikh extremists in order to counterbalance Sikh moderates and their party, the Akali Dal, which had come to power in Punjab in 1977, defeating the Congress Party there. As a consequence of the Emergency, she had been in a political wilderness between 1977 and 1980. Once back in office, she hoped that the Sikhs' house, divided against itself, would fall and the Congress Party return to power in the state. But the Sikh extremists got out of control.

Ten million of the country's fourteen million Sikhs lived in Punjab, but so did more than nine million Hindus. Sikh extremists, after murdering Hindus and burning their houses and shops, took refuge in Sikh temples, where they could be sure of not being pursued, for not only were a majority of the officials and police in the state Sikhs but also it was the central government's policy, at the time, not to pursue armed extremists into a temple. The Punjab government was not able to control the violence, and moderate Sikhs everywhere, torn between loyalty to their religion and a wish to live and work in a secular state in which they enjoyed all the rights of the majority, did not denounce the extremists or dissociate themselves from them. (Their silence became a lasting grievance among the Hindus.) Mrs. Gandhi allowed the Punjab situation to deteriorate, and finally, in October of 1983, she dismissed the state government and put the state under President's Rule.

There are moments in politics that reverberate in time like a perpetually tolling bell, and when that happens the significance of the moment often cannot be assessed until long after the tolling has begun. For instance, in 1919 the British government passed the Rowlatt Act, which kept in force in India such wartime emergency measures as press censorship and summary justice for political agitators. Indian nationalist feeling was so strongly aroused by the act that Mahatma Gandhi called a twenty-four-hour nationwide general strike to protest it. Almost as soon as the strike was launched, it degenerated into a national riot, which continued for days and claimed many lives. Amritsar, then in the British province of the Punjab, was the scene of the worst rioting. One day, a mob there assaulted an English schoolteacher, and she barely escaped with her life. The next day, Brigadier General Reginald Dyer arrived to restore order. The following day, he proclaimed a ban on all public meetings and processions. The day after that, in defiance of his ban, some five thousand residents of Amritsar held a meeting at Jallianwalla Bagh, a mostly walled-in tract of land in the center of the city. General Dyer blocked the main entrance with troops and ordered them to open fire. Within ten minutes, at least four hundred entrapped, unarmed people were killed and twelve hundred maimed or wounded. Over the subsequent twenty-eight years of Indian struggle for independence, the Jallianwalla Bagh massacre—though it was exceptional in the history of the British raj—became a byword for British brutality. Many historians now believe that the memory of it was partly responsible for the inability of the nationalists to work out with the British some kind of self-rule formula for India in the course of the next two decades. If they had done so, India might have gained independence peacefully in the nineteen-thirties and been spared the ravages of the Hindu-Muslim conflict and the Partition, which in the Punjab alone left eleven million people homeless and a million dead.

In June, 1984, in the new, truncated state of Punjab, the democratically elected government of Mrs. Indira Gandhi went the Rowlatt Act one better. It suspended publication of all local newspapers, expelled all foreigners, barred all foreign correspondents, imposed curfews on all the state's cities, cut off all rail and bus service, and banned all non-military vehicles from the roads. It reinforced the Army in Punjab and gave it orders to move troops into Amritsar, the holy city of the Sikhs. In Amritsar, the troops were ordered to shoot any curfew-breaker on sight and to flush out the Sikh extremist Jarnail Singh Bhindranwale, some of the other prominent Sikh extremists, and those of their followers who had been living for months in the precincts of the Golden Temple, which is only a short distance from Jallianwalla Bagh. Despite the press blackout, it soon became clear from official and unofficial reports that on June 6th, in an operation code-named Blue Star, no fewer than six battalions, armed with tanks and heavy artillery, stormed and seized the Golden Temple, which the Sikh extremists had turned into a virtual military fortress, and that they fought Bhindranwale and his followers, who had armed themselves with machine guns, rockets, and anti-tank missiles for just such a holy battle. The engagement lasted forty-eight hours and left perhaps two hundred and fifty soldiers and a thousand of the extremists, including Bhindranwale, dead, with possibly as many, on both sides, maimed or wounded. In the attack, some of the temple buildings were extensively damaged. Operation Blue Star had the unintended effect of making martyrs of the Sikh extremist "marchers"—and especially of Bhindranwale, at best, an eccentric monk—whom a majority of the Sikhs had until then disowned as fanatics. In fact, it radicalized the Sikhs and fanned the demand for a separate homeland.

In the battle, the stakes for Mrs. Gandhi's government had been high. Unlike Christians or Muslims or any of the other minorities, Sikhs were at the center of Indian politics, business, and national power. Some of the most prosperous people in the big cities were Sikhs. Although most Sikhs were businessmen, officials, farmers, mechanics, drivers, or shopkeepers, some Sikhs held important positions in the Army, of which Sikhs formed a significant part. (The exact number is classified.) Eighty per cent of the Sikhs were concentrated in Punjab, which is India's breadbasket and the home of its "green revolution," and supplies food to many poorer states. (Some said that a Sikh threat to block the transport of food from Punjab to other states was what ultimately goaded Mrs. Gandhi into attacking the Golden Temple.) Moreover, Punjab is strategically situated—between New Delhi and Pakistan, India's greatest enemy, and between New Delhi and the state of Jammu and Kashmir, over which India and Pakistan had already fought two wars. Amritsar is near what has turned out to be the quite porous border with Pakistan. Sikhs were able to smuggle in arms from Pakistan, and possibly even receive training in guerrilla tactics there, thus "destabilizing the Indian government," as officials put it.

The Sikhs' struggle for some kind of autonomy—there seemed to be no consensus among them on just what they wanted—soon began to be spoken of by Sikhs, in characteristic hyperbole, as "the holy battle of the turban against the cap." Their turban, they said, was worn boldly over their Samson-like unshorn hair, while the cap covered the shaved skull of the Hindu. (In actuality, only some ascetic Hindus shave their heads. The rhetoric also ignored facts such as that the turban was probably introduced to India by the Moguls, that some Hindus wear turbans every day and many Hindus wear them on ceremonial occasions, and that threatening to take someone's turban off is an insult among Sikhs and Hindus alike.) According to the Sikhs, the turban stands tall and majestic on top of a Sikh's head, while the cap lies squat and common on the Hindu head. "How can a cap have dominion over the turban?" a young Sikh in New Delhi asked me. "When has the turban ever bowed to a cap?" And he added, "We must have our Khalistan." In a study of India's Sikh problem for the London-based Minority Rights Group, the English scholar Christopher Shackle wrote of the man who was perhaps the strongest advocate of Khalistan, "In life, much of Bhindranwale's appeal lay in his power to articulate forcefully the easily invoked extreme solutions to minority status that might be reached by open fighting between the Sikh turban and the Hindu cap." He went on to quote this passage from one of Bhindranwale's typically confusing speeches:

It is a matter of keeping the unshorn hair, the beard, and the sword-belt. The Sikhs are a separate nation. Some say we are separate already. If so, then why say we are second-class citizens? That the Sikhs are historically separate even the cap-people have admitted. But if Bhindranwale proclaims this, they say that what he wants is Khalistan. We have endured enough slavery over the past thirty-six years. Now, no matter how many heads may roll, we must be free.

Seeing the conflict in terms of the turban and the cap may seem absurd, but history abounds in examples of people fighting for symbols, people laying waste whole kingdoms for the cross of the Christians or the crescent of Islam. The turban and the cap might be only latter-day Indian versions of the aristocratic curly locks of the Cavaliers and the plebeian short hair of the Roundheads in seventeenth-century England. Still, it boggles the mind to think that the survival of India as a united country might depend on the outcome of such a conflict of symbols.

Sikhs started saying that Sikhism, "the religion of the turban," had an aggressive, masculine character, because it was monotheistic, worshipping the god Truth; they said contemptuously that, in contrast, Hinduism, "the religion of the cap," had a pacific, feminine character, because it was polytheistic. The Hindus, in general, rejected the Sikhs' characterization of them indignantly but did grudgingly acknowledge that Sikhs are "a martial people" with "a martial history." Indeed, in some respects Sikh males do appear more "masculine" than their Hindu counterparts, perhaps because of the external marks of the beard and mustache, the steel bracelet, and the sabre. Certainly the surname Singh both adds to the Sikh men's sense of masculinity and makes of them a sort of brotherhood.

It was hard to underestimate the importance, somewhere deep in the Sikh mind, of the fact that it was a woman who stormed and seized the citadel of the Sikhs' masculine, martial religion. A woman not only dared to penetrate the Sikhs' sanctum sanctorum but, in the course of the assault, damaged it. She might as well have stamped on the Sikh turban, demoted the lion to the status of a goat. The humiliation was all the greater because she had a Sikh general, other Sikh officers, and Sikh soldiers take part in the attack. After the storming of the temple, Sikh women taunted their menfolk with remarks like "The Hindus have taken the starch out of your mustache."

Mrs. Gandhi was, of course, fully aware of the distinctive character of the Sikhs. In 1982, she could almost certainly have defused the extremist movement by engaging in negotiation and making some strategic concessions to the moderates. Failing that, she could have forcibly cleared Bhindranwale and his followers out of the Golden Temple before they had a chance to amass arms and, with the collusion of Sikh police in Punjab, turn it into a military camp. Even at the eleventh hour, she could have instructed her troops not to shoot their way into the temple but to lay siege to it—cut off supplies of food and water, and starve the extremists out. (This was, in fact, the course that the government of Prime Minister Narasimha Rao took in Srinagar, Kashmir, in 1993, on being confronted with armed Muslims who had barricaded themselves in the Hazratbal Mosque, which is considered especially sacred because it is the repository of a strand of hair said to be from the head of Muhammad.) But in Amritsar that approach might have taken weeks, or even months, and given the extremists a chance to publicize their demands, and might have left her with the embarrassing need to make them political prisoners. (Jails in India have proved even better political platforms than temples.) Besides, such measures might have provoked a more general Sikh rebellion in Punjab, since the Sikh masses there venerated as saints the Sikh leaders whom the government branded terrorists and murderers. But moderate Sikhs maintain that in this way she would have respected the sanctity of the temple and not given offense to the honor and dignity of the Sikh male. They say that the fundamentalist movement in Punjab was so strong that for them to have spoken out against it would have been to commit political suicide. They point to the fundamentalist movement sweeping through Islamic countries—Iran in particular—and ask which Iranian Muslim was able to stand up to Ayatollah Khomeini and his zealots and live. They say that Operation Blue Star made them even more helpless than they were before.

Anyway, Mrs. Gandhi, as she had often done before, chose a military solution to a political problem—this time, perhaps, because she calculated that her crackdown on the Sikhs would win her more Hindu votes in the next general election, which she was constitutionally required to hold before the end of January, 1985. But by that choice she certainly alienated practically all Sikhs and laid the foundation for a guerrilla war in Punjab. Moreover, she divided the Army against itself by fostering mutiny in its Sikh contingent: after Operation Blue Star, there were widespread desertions and mutinies of Sikhs in the Army. A number of the deserters headed toward Punjab—some, like their civilian brothers, to make a pilgrimage to Amritsar, and others to sow seeds of revenge against Mrs. Gandhi's government. There were reports of gun battles between officers and soldiers, and of the pursuit and arrest of Sikh deserters. Thus, it could be that Mrs. Gandhi permanently hobbled the Army, tarnishing the integrity of the one institution in independent India that had remained beyond reproach. It had been the greatest instrument of law and order in a country seething with factional strife, and the greatest exemplar of the ethnic unity that Mrs. Gandhi's father and Mahatma Gandhi, the spiritual father of the nation, had tried to forge. The spilling of the blood at the temple had tragic consequences for Mrs. Gandhi, and the tolling of the bell of the battle continues to reverberate through the country.

Because of the censorship surrounding Operation Blue Star, most people in Punjab and the rest of the country were initially kept in the dark about the battle of the Golden Temple, but soon afterward Mrs. Gandhi's government tried to pacify the Sikh community with assurances that, contrary to rumor, the Golden Temple proper was not destroyed or defaced; indeed, it went as far as to circulate pictures of the temple taken after the battle. Rumor, however, has great power in India. Mrs. Gandhi's career was almost ended in 1977 when people at large confused the unfamiliar birth-control measure of vasectomy, promoted by Sanjay, with castration, which was familiar from the procedure used on bulls in rural India.

Though Mrs. Gandhi spent tens of millions of rupees restoring the damaged temple buildings and went to the Golden Temple to pray, she showed no remorse for Operation Blue Star. She claimed that the Sikhs themselves were responsible for the desecration of their temple, pointing to evidence that since August of 1982 Sikh extremists had been arming themselves and taking sanctuary not only in the Golden Temple but also in other Punjabi temples, and that Bhindranwale and his followers had used the Golden Temple to traffic illegally in arms and to carry out assassinations, creating conditions that made Punjab ungovernable for her. She suggested that the Sikh extremists were no different from the tribal groups who over the years had been waging guerrilla warfare in the jungles and mountains of northeastern India. And she excoriated moderate Sikhs for not dissociating themselves from the extremists—for not putting their own house in order and thus obviating the need for her military action.

But Mrs. Gandhi knew as well as anyone that victory in the battle for the Golden Temple would be Pyrrhic. Sikhs were famous for their long-running vendettas. It was certain that they would not rest until they had avenged the desecration of the temple, and that some of them would regard it as their religious duty to take her life. By contrast, she, in her dealings with Sikhs, would be under all kinds of constraints. At the time she sent the Army into the Golden Temple, she repeatedly stressed the fact that she was striking not against the Sikh religion but only against the Sikh extremists. The distinction, if it was to have meaning, required her to treat all other

54

Sikhs—the Sikh President of the country, the Sikh members of her Cabinet, the Sikhs in her bodyguard—as she would treat any loyal citizens. Although, as a precaution, Sikhs were removed from her bodyguard four days after the assault, they were restored to it a week or so later, for if there had been the perception that she was keeping Sikhs at a distance she would, by implication, have accused all Sikhs of disloyalty and indubitably alienated all the Sikh moderates, whose friendship and good will she needed in order to rule— to keep the nation whole.

There was something especially poignant in the fact that, on October 31st, a little over four months after the attack on the Golden Temple, Mrs. Gandhi was killed by two Sikhs who were members of her bodyguard. Her father and she—who, between them, had by then ruled India for thirty-three of the thirty-seven years of its independent life—were committed to a secular state, in which all religions, sects, and creeds could flourish. They had lived through the Partition of India, and they feared that if there should be another rent the whole fabric of the young country might fall apart. Yet Mrs. Gandhi, perhaps the shrewdest politician her young nation has produced, must have known even before she gave the Army its orders that Sikhs forced to choose between the call of their religion and the obligation to protect her—however strong their loyalty to her person—would choose religion. And the call to avenge what the Sikhs perceived as the desecration of their temple went out from some Sikh religious leaders at almost the moment the Army entered the temple precincts. Mrs. Gandhi knew that after the call she might not be able to count on even those Sikhs who were moderates.

Following the assault on the Golden Temple, the government included commandos in the circle of Mrs. Gandhi's bodyguard, and in the bodyguard of Rajiv and his wife and children. But it was a futile gesture, because the Sikhs in her bodyguard were still—as they had always been—only a step away from her. Though she was the unquestioned leader of seven hundred million people, she was helpless, and it seemed that she knew she might be killed at any time. A few days before she died, she said to a BBC television reporter, "Well, I've lived with danger all my life, and I think I've had a pretty full life, and it makes no difference whether you die in bed or you die standing up."

Mrs. Gandhi was walking from her house to her office in her compound when she was struck down. By her violent death, she became a political martyr. The one of her two assassins who was gunned down on the spot became a Sikh martyr. There was much speculation about why Mrs. Gandhi acted in a way that made her assassination at the hands of a Sikh almost a foregone conclusion. Even as she decided on her action, she must have heard the echoes of the murder in the cathedral—the murder of Thomas à Becket by the henchmen of Henry II—which had resonated in Western literature for eight centuries; she had probably read T. S. Eliot's play about the murder and perhaps seen the film based on Jean Anouilh's play. People who saw her regularly in the later years of her rule said that after the death of Sanjay she seemed to lose her zest for living. At the time of Operation Blue Star, she was sixty-six. She had led the country for nearly sixteen years, all told, and during most of those years she had got a bad press. She talked as if she were bruised and tired. She stood on the brink of a general election for which all the portents were against her. People said that, having arranged for her surviving child to succeed her, she might well have decided, in some part of her mind, that it was time to pass the torch.

Following the news of Mrs. Gandhi's assassination, Hindus in New Delhi and a dozen other cities went on a rampage, beating up and killing Sikhs and burning Sikh houses, shops, and vehicles. In the anti-Sikh rioting, which raged for four days and nights, at least three thousand Sikhs were killed and twenty-five thousand left homeless in Delhi alone. Many Hindu politicians, who had no use for the spirit of religious toleration that Mrs. Gandhi, her father, and other Congress leaders had been trying to cultivate since the Partition, actively promoted the riots. They were a portent of what could happen to Sikhs living outside Punjab if a Sikh nation came into being and a full-scale exodus of Hindus from Punjab occurred: those Sikhs, who were among the most prosperous people in the country, would lose everything.

What was especially alarming about this convulsion of Hindu violence against the Sikhs was that it was surprisingly voiceless: no Hindus spoke up on radio or television or in the newspapers to say that they held the Sikh community responsible for the act of the two Sikh assassins; nor did anyone come forward to contradict the generally accepted view that Hindus and Sikhs had lived together amicably for four hundred years, and that the violence of the Sikh extremists in Punjab in the early eighties was an exception. Consequently, the causes of the violence against the Sikhs were the subject of much speculation by observers of it—by the government officials charged with controlling it, and the Western journalists who rushed in to report on it. The speculation concentrated on political, social, and religious causes. It was said that Mrs. Gandhi's very personal style of government had eroded the structure of the ruling party, so that the party bosses had become increasingly dependent on *goondas,* or thugs, to keep the party in power through intimidation and extortion, and that the *goondas* used the opportunity of the assassination to whip up anti-Sikh sentiment in the hope of winning right-wing Hindu votes in the coming general election. It was said that for some time the law-and-order situation in India had been deteriorating, with the result that many neighborhoods and cities were at the mercy of *goonda* rule, and that the *goondas* used the opportunity of the assassination to kill Sikhs and to loot Sikh homes and shops. It was said that Hindu religious passions stirred up by the assassination boiled over. No doubt there was a modicum of truth in that speculation. Political, social, and religious tinder is ever present in Indian society, and just a spark can ignite it.

In any event, the outbreak of communal violence gave the impression that the machinery of law and order had broken down completely and the government had lost control. Several citizens' groups subsequently looked into the pattern of the violence and concluded that, except for a few burnings of Sikh vehicles and the manhandling of some Sikhs in the neighborhood of the hospital to which the wounded Mrs. Gandhi was rushed, the violence was not spontaneous, did not even stem from the Hindus' grief and anguish at the death of their Prime Minister, but was politically inspired. According to these citizens' groups, some leaders of the ruling Congress Party made anonymous telephone calls spreading false rumors in New Delhi: Sikhs have poisoned the city's water supply; Sikhs have killed all the Hindu passengers on the train from Punjab; Sikh marauders are killing Hindus in the city. Some of the politicians, the groups said, trucked in professional hooligans from outlying villages and then, using voters' lists, pointed out to the assembled mobs Sikh houses for burning.

Yet the more the violence was explained the more incomprehensible it seemed. One moment, there was no mob; Hindus and Sikhs were living side by side along a back lane, sharing a single water tap, buying from and selling to each other. The next moment, the same Hindus were killing their Sikh neighbors and setting fire to the neighbors' homes and shops. The mob, as the world has lately come to realize, can seem to function more like a natural phenomenon, like a hurricane or a volcano, than like a human phenomenon, in which people weigh risks and rewards. In this place or that, it lashes and disappears, it erupts and subsides, without saying what it wants, what it needs, how those needs can be satisfied, how the aroused passions can be checked. The spectre hanging over India of this mob violence, whose victims one day were Sikhs but another day could be Hindus or Muslims, Nagas or Assamese, Untouchables or Brahmans, Bengalis or Biharis, South Indians or North Indians, or any of a thousand other groups or communities living in uncertain peace, is what poses the greatest threat to the survival of the much battered Indian Union.

3

Rajiv's Political Honeymoon

Congress Indira leaders, after anointing Rajiv as Mrs. Gandhi's successor within hours of her death, apparently decided that only a quick general election could give political legitimacy to what was essentially a dynastic succession. Rajiv—as he was called even after he became Prime Minister—shared this view and immediately advanced by a month the date of the general election scheduled for late January, 1985. His action insured that he would be the beneficiary not only of the sympathy vote but also of the anti-Sikh vote. The Congress Indira leaders felt that if they created an atmosphere of Hindu solidarity they could capture the right-wing Hindu vote, which generally went to the opposition parties. Apparently, the lesser Congress Indira politicians, sensing this strategy, had hurriedly arranged the four-day anti-Sikh riots, to help Rajiv win and, at the same time, to teach the Sikhs a lesson. (A member of Parliament who was thought to have instigated the anti-Sikh violence, Lalit Maken, was gunned down, presumably by Sikhs, in July, 1985, with his wife, in front of their house in New Delhi.)

In the general election, Rajiv ran as Mr. Clean, a powerful symbol in a society mired in poverty and political corruption. On campaign posters, he was sometimes portrayed holding a broom, the broom being associated with the ancient institution of Untouchability and with the sweepers who for thousands of years have

Rajiv Gandhi. New Delhi, ca. 1988. (S. K. Chadha.)

swept up India's human filth and muck. But, as newspapers pointed out, although Rajiv talked at the hustings about modernizing India and getting it ready for the twenty-first century, he still sometimes spoke as if the threat of Sikh secession were the only issue before the country—a ploy to get the right-wing Hindu vote. In any event, he routed the opposition and won for his party its biggest victory in independent India, chalking up a greater number of votes than had ever been garnered by either his mother or his grandfather, and securing eighty per cent of the seats in the Lok Sabha, the lower house of Parliament. The general election left no doubt that he had been given a national mandate.

From the very beginning, Rajiv seemed to be interested in new departures. Unlike his predecessors, he seemed to believe that rapid economic development was a matter not merely of devising good socialist programs but of improving the management of the programs and creating a more hospitable atmosphere for private industry. Over the years, he must have heard from many of his boarding-school friends who had gone into private business how socialist-inspired government controls made private industry inefficient; as a pilot for the government's Indian Airlines for fourteen years, he had experienced its notorious inefficiencies at first hand. Whereas his mother had tried to advance the economy mostly by means of Soviet-style planning, he seemed determined to get faster results by using the technological achievements of the West. Whereas during much of her rule she had tightened governmental controls in the service of socialist principles—she had nationalized banks, abolished the privy purses of the princes, taken over the coal mines, and tried to guarantee prices for farmers and establish a nationwide distribution system for grain—he set about loosening the controls. And, in contrast to his mother's aggressive public-relations style, his had a certain softness. (His youthful looks and aristocratic bearing attracted publicity nationally and worldwide. In photographs of international conferences, such as the Commonwealth Conferences, he stood out among the Asian and African leaders—he might almost have been an Englishman—and the photographs were reprinted widely in India.) Above all, he abandoned his mother's policy of confrontation and emphasized reconciliation.

Although Rajiv had not been directly associated with the decision to invade the Golden Temple, he inherited the Sikh problem, which was perhaps his mother's worst legacy. Along with every other Hindu in India, he had to find a way of living and working with the Sikhs. After the election, Rajiv did an about-face. He tried to distance himself from his mother's policies against the Sikh extremists—indeed, from his own campaign pronouncements—and went to great lengths to clear the air of communal suspicion and hostility. He let it be known almost at the outset that he was open to any compromise solution to the Sikh problem as long as it did not threaten the integrity and unity of the country. He released Sikh leaders and Sikh extremists who had been summarily arrested during the last months of his mother's regime, when Punjab was placed under martial law. And he went as far as to initiate an official investigation into the anti-Sikh riots, even though it was probably his ox that would be gored.

Many observers thought that the Prime Ministership of Rajiv Gandhi would ultimately fly or founder on the basis of how he was able to solve the Sikh problem. The solution to that problem, however, lay not so much with him as with the Sikhs themselves. The riots had given the Sikhs the scare of their lives, and had made them distrustful of Hindus and distrustful of living in India. Sikhs acquired the look of hunted animals. The Sikh doormen who once adorned the entrances of hotels and offices in New Delhi as proudly as if they were the gatekeepers of the country skulked around wearing bitter, wounded expressions. Any of them who were asked their views of Mrs. Gandhi or Rajiv were apt to say things like "Sikh arms and legs are swelling up with poison."

The extremist Sikhs appeared to be inventing legend and calling it history, and then acting on it as if they were being propelled by something real rather than something imagined; for instance, they spoke about Operation Blue Star as "the biggest blow struck against the Sikh nation," as if Mrs. Gandhi's sacrilege were the worst insult in Sikh history. Actually, that history includes examples of worse insults: in the eighteenth century, the Afghans had twice blown up the Golden Temple and, in one battle, had killed twenty thousand Sikhs, in an attempt to crush Sikhism and Sikh military power. The extremists, however, with their propaganda of "the biggest blow," so stirred up the Sikh masses that Sikh leaders were initially reluctant to parley with Rajiv, for fear that their support would melt away like a cake of ghi in the sun. Again, the extremists referred to the government in New Delhi as the Delhi throne, as if the democratically elected Indian government were another Mogul or British imperium. Sikhs were famous for their wars against the Moguls and the British, and the extremists had apparently convinced themselves that they were fighting a similar war against the Indian government. Again, they said that Hindus had always been untrustworthy, pointing to the case of a Brahman cook who in Mogul times supposedly betrayed the sons of one of their gurus to the Muslims. So now they took to murdering Hindus. And they now talked about "the Sikh religion" and "Sikh interests," as if these had always been in opposition to the religion and the interests of the Hindus, forgetting that the founder of Sikhism, Guru Nanak (1469–1539), was a Hindu, that the Sikhs' nine subsequent gurus were all Hindus, that all the gurus belonged to the same Hindu warrior caste, that all the early Sikhs were originally Hindus, and that, historically, Sikhs were the protectors of Hindus—their "sword arm." The tradition of Sikhs being the protectors was so strong that a Punjabi Hindu family would often bring up its eldest son as a Sikh and change his surname to Singh. In the past, Sikhs and Hindus were so close that intermarriages were common, and the Sikh scriptures were treated as part of the body of the Hindus' sacred writings.

Rajiv Gandhi and Rama's Kingdom

Almost the first act of Rajiv as Prime Minister was to stop the anti-Sikh riots from spreading, by quick and forceful government response. He set in motion the machinery for investigating and punishing the instigators, and he followed that move up by initiating talks with the president of the Akali Dal, Harchand Singh Longowal, who had been in the Golden Temple at the time of the assault.

In what was seen by political observers as an act of personal courage, Longowal, on July 24, 1985, reached an accord with Rajiv and his Cabinet, after thirty-three hours of continuous talks. In it Rajiv acceded to many of the Sikh extremists' political demands: Chandigarh was to become the capital solely of Punjab in January, 1986; official commissions were to make recommendations on what land from Punjab would be awarded to Haryana for its loss of Chandigarh and on what compensation the innocent victims of the violence in Punjab since August of 1982 should receive; a judicial tribunal was to decide on the distribution of the Ravi and Beas river waters. Longowal, too, seemed to make some concessions. He stated that the Akali Dal's Anandpur Sahib resolutions of 1981 and 1983 were not intended to undermine the Union. In the words of the accord, "the purpose of the Resolution is to provide greater autonomy to the State with a view to strengthening the unity and integrity of the country, since unity in diversity forms the cornerstone of our national entity." Ironically, the accord was essentially the same as one that had been proposed by a group of Hindu and Sikh intellectuals to Mrs. Gandhi in September, 1983; she had rejected it, because she had seen it as the first step toward a Sikh nation and dissolution of the union.

In a sense, Rajiv's and Longowal's accord settled nothing—only postponed dealing with most of the difficult issues in the Anandpur Sahib resolutions. Both sides seemed to take refuge in commissions and rhetorical formulas. Still, Rajiv had parleyed with an extremist private citizen almost as if the citizen represented a government, and that parley had been conciliatory in spirit and obviously preferable to his mother's military solution. The accord immediately came under attack by leaders of Rajiv's own party—especially those from the neighboring states of Haryana and Rajasthan. And, although Longowal won the Akali Dal Party's acceptance of it in a meeting in Anandpur Sahib on July 26th, its reception among the Sikhs was lukewarm or outright hostile. His key lieutenants—Prakash Singh Badal, the former Akali chief minister of Punjab, and Gurcharan Singh Tohra, the president of the Sikhs' temple-management committee, which is the greatest repository of Sikh priestly power (it controls, among other things, the purse strings of the Sikh temples)—initially withheld their approval, perhaps because they had been left out of the negotiations. The Sikhs who had been followers of Bhindranwale—they had been led since his death by Bhindranwale's eighty-four-year-old father, Joginder Singh—condemned the agreement as a "sellout." But then they had had little use for Longowal since Operation Blue Star: unlike the "martyred Bhindranwale," he had surrendered to Mrs. Gandhi's Army at the Golden Temple.

Right after reaching the accord, Rajiv hurriedly called elections in Punjab for late September, 1985. He did so against the advice of Longowal, who had risked repudiation by the Sikhs there for merely holding talks with Rajiv and wanted time to sell the accord to them. Apparently, Rajiv couldn't wait to hand over the administration of Punjab to the Sikhs and make them responsible for dealing with the extremists. On August 20th, Longowal was shot dead in the village of Sherpur, in Punjab, by a band of extremists. His death was seen as a political tragedy, since without his statesmanship the enforcement of the accord, the neutralization of the extremists, and the holding of elections in Punjab—Rajiv's whole policy of finding a quick solution to the Sikh problem—were put in doubt.

Observers noted that whether Rajiv would eventually be able

to bring peace to Punjab would depend on the continuing effect on Sikh politics of Operation Blue Star. That action had been applauded by the Indian newspapers, but at the time the Sikh historian and novelist Khushwant Singh had said of it, "What the Akalis failed to achieve by persuasion and agitation may be achieved by the events of June 6, 1984," and "Far from crushing the Khalistan movement, it has given it the sustenance it lacked and weakened the hands of Sikhs like me who are bitterly opposed to it." (He himself had once been an advocate of a Sikh homeland.) The elections did go forward, and they brought to power a new Akali Dal government, whose chief minister was Surjit Singh Barnala, but it was faction-ridden from the start. Some of its most important members soon defected, and one, Prakash Singh Badal, formed a breakaway Akali Dal Party, with himself as its president. Because each member of the government tried to appear more devout than the next, none of them were able to take action against the extremists, who had had allies among the Sikh priests all along—including the powerful Gurcharan Singh Tohra. Tohra had been reëlected president of the temple-management committee and had, like Badal, been busy undermining the Barnala government. (Later, both were put in jail for their activities.)

Barnala himself had very little room to maneuver—caught, as he was, between the demands of Rajiv's government and those of his own religion. The Golden Temple was once again occupied by Sikh extremists, and on April 29th they formally proclaimed from its sanctuary their aim of establishing an independent Sikh nation. The Barnala government had no choice but to use the state police to clear them out. This created such a backlash from Sikhs of every stripe that Barnala had to do penance by visiting various Sikh temples for a week and, like an Untouchable, cleaning the shoes of every worshipper who came and went. The accord was a dead letter: Chandigarh continued to be the capital of both states, for the question of compensation for Haryana remained stuck in Sikh-Hindu politics. Meanwhile, audiocassettes recounting in song and verse the heroic deeds of Bhindranwale and other martyred Sikh extremists were being openly sold around Sikh temples for fifteen or twenty rupees, about a third the price of other cassettes in the marketplace. These cassettes, which also included homilies and verses from Sikh scriptures recited by priests, had the authority of religious appeal, and the extremists were disseminating them from village to village in Punjab. Rajiv seemed to be losing the propaganda battle almost without having joined it.

There were daily reports of Sikh extremists rampaging through Punjab, killing Hindus and hiding in temples; of Hindus in Punjab being unable to sell their property to go to live elsewhere, as if the Sikhs thought it only a matter of time before the property would be theirs; and of Hindu refugees arriving in neighboring states. There were also frequent reports of extremists shooting down important Punjab officials, hijacking buses and killing the Hindu passengers, and randomly firing into Hindu and Sikh crowds—all acts intended to create mass terror. In October, some extremists wore police uniforms to get past security guards in Punjab and fire at officials. The ruse created a new sense of panic, because anyone in uniform had routinely been able to get in practically anywhere in India. Likewise, the assassination in August of General Arun S. Vaidya, a retired Army chief of staff, who was India's most decorated soldier, and who had supervised the Golden Temple attack but had since retired to the city of Pune, about a thousand miles from Punjab, raised the question of how anyone who had been a public servant and had taken a public stand against the Sikh extremists could ever hope to live a normal private life. The extremists' strategy seemed to be to provoke a Hindu backlash in the country at large in order to radicalize the rest of the Sikhs— to step up the level of violence and make all attempts at compromise futile. Their strategy worked. In August, they goaded Rajiv's government into passing legislation that gave the central government special military powers to deal with the "disturbed" areas. And Mrs. Gandhi's assassins, whom the Sikhs regarded as heroes, were sentenced to death. Her policy of retribution was reinstated with a vengeance.

Rajiv Gandhi and Rama's Kingdom

Rajiv Gandhi was born on August 20, 1944, in Bombay. When he was small, Mrs. Gandhi and her husband, Feroze, began living separately, and Mrs. Gandhi moved in with her father, in the Prime Minister's house. It was there that Rajiv grew up, under the care of a Danish nurse. He went to Doon School, in Dehra Dun, in the foothills of the Himalayas—a school modelled on British public schools, and one of the two or three most expensive private schools in the country. Rajiv was known there more for taking part in sports and going on hikes than for his studies, but he got a place at Trinity College, Cambridge—Nehru's alma mater—to study mechanical sciences. He was there for almost three years, between 1962 and 1965, but the authorities apparently informed his family that he was not a suitable candidate for a degree. The family, using its influence, got him admitted into Imperial College, of London University, to study mechanical engineering, but the authorities there reached the same conclusion as those at Cambridge, and after a year he returned home without taking an examination or receiving a degree. Official biographies, however, routinely list him as having received a Bachelor of Science and a Master of Arts from Cambridge; in the British *Who's Who,* he was listed as having received both degrees in the very year that the Trinity College records show him to have enrolled there. In New Delhi, he joined the local flying club, eventually obtained a commercial pilot's license, and then became a pilot with Indian Airlines.

In 1968, Rajiv married Sonia Maino; he had met her in Cambridge, where she had been taking an English-language course for foreign students at a local school. In the next few years, they had two children—Rahul, in 1971, and Priyanka, in 1972. (Official biographies disagree on the children's exact dates of birth.) Rajiv seemed to be the first member of the Gandhi-Nehru clan to have a happy family life, and observers said that this had some bearing on why he had kept out of politics so long, even though he and his family lived with his mother in the Prime Minister's house. (It is known, though, that he opposed the Emergency and that he also objected to Sanjay's ruthless political methods.) After Sanjay was killed, Rajiv entered politics almost as a family duty, but he was so inept at making speeches and presiding over public occasions—in Sanjay's constituency of Amethi, for instance—that, although he won Sanjay's old seat there, few thought he had the mettle to become a national leader in his own right. He mastered public speaking quickly, however, and even learned to work the crowds. And when he became Prime Minister there was general euphoria. For one thing, when the Party leaders elected him to fill his mother's office he conducted himself with a grace and dignity that helped make the transition to his rule smooth and peaceful. In addition, he was young; unlike so many other politicians, he was not hostage to any regional or other special-interest groups; and, unlike his mother, he was at ease with himself and with the world. Politicians who went to see him were struck by the quiet, quick way he did business. Everyone who had dealings with him found him to be decent, direct, unassuming, and modest, and remarked on how courteous he was: he called his mother's old advisers "Sir" and escorted visitors to the door. Such qualities stood out in a political atmosphere of unbridled arrogance and abject sycophancy.

Personally, he seemed to have a taste for good living. Certainly he had a passion for fine clothes. Until he entered politics and had to appear to be a man of the people, he was often seen wearing designer jeans, Gucci shoes, a Cartier watch, and imported sunglasses. He did not wear the cloth cap associated with men of the Congress, and he shunned garlands and other symbolic badges of Indian politicians. (Sonia was known for elegant shoes and bags and for an interest in fashion.) He also enjoyed good food. Before he became Prime Minister, he and Sonia were often seen at Casa Medici, a restaurant serving Continental fare in the luxurious Taj Hotel, or at the Orient Express, in the newer and even more luxurious Taj Palace Hotel. At home, they ate Indian and Continental food. He had a sweet tooth and a taste for colas; on his travels around the country, he was apt to stop his cavalcade of cars to pick up some sweets or a soft drink. He liked target-shooting; he had had a gun license for years, and one of his prized possessions was his father's gun. Among his other hobbies were photography, electronics, and ham radio. He also kept parrots that talked. But perhaps his greatest love was music, of all varieties; he was known to have one of the best stereo systems in the country.

After becoming Prime Minister, Rajiv moved out of his mother's house (what had been the Prime Minister's official residence was named the Indira Gandhi Memorial Museum) and into two heavily guarded government bungalows nearby. Prime Ministers used to go about in open cars, mix freely with crowds, and disdain all forms of security as being natural to dictatorships but unnatural to democracies. Rajiv and his family, however, were kept cordoned off; except for a close circle of trusted friends, they saw hardly anybody socially. Rajiv wore a bulletproof vest, and he made his trips in one of a group of identical cars, so that no one could know which car he was travelling in. And every time he went out, it was said, hundreds of policemen in the city were alerted. Even so, the security measures were not immune to Indian inefficiency. In October of 1986, there was a nearly successful attempt on Rajiv's life while he was at Mahatma Gandhi's cremation ground, attending a prayer ceremony to mark the Mahatma's hundred-and-seventeenth birthday: a would-be assassin fired two or three times from the bushes, and Rajiv's security guards dismissed the first shot as the backfiring of a scooter.

It was said that since Mrs. Gandhi's attack on the Golden Temple the Gandhi name had become anathema to Sikh extremists, and that no one bearing that name would ever be safe again—that if Rajiv Gandhi had not been the Prime Minister, with the entire power of the state protecting him, he and his family might have already been eliminated. Immediately after the attack, it was reported that the Gandhi children were on the extremists' hit list. At the time, Rahul was at Doon School, and Priyanka was at Welham, its sister school. They were taken out of school and brought back to New Delhi, and thereafter they studied at home, seeing only the children of the family friends who were allowed inside the Prime Minister's house. They had to grow up in an abnormal, claustrophobic environment, without the benefit of team sports or the emotional nourishment provided by informal social contacts. Both were approaching college age, and that exacerbated the problem of their education, because it was taken for granted that they would be no more safe from Sikh vengeance in a college in the West than in a college in India. But with the passage of time the threat seemed to diminish, and today they are safe and well.

New Delhi itself gave the impression of being a city under siege. The south block of the Secretariat, where the most important government officials had their offices, was guarded by specially trained forces, and security guards protected not only many politicians, officials, and ex-officials but also many journalists. Security guards armed with Sten guns were permanently posted in front of the house of Khushwant Singh. In the past, he had travelled all over the world regularly, but after the troubles of the nineteen-eighties, because of the danger to his life, he did not go out very much. Similarly, three prominent Hindu journalists in New Delhi who at one time or another had taken anti-Sikh-extremist stands were guarded around the clock, each being supplied with a contingent of about fifteen government security guards, also armed with Sten guns. One of the three, Arun Shourie, told me there was such a climate of fear in the land that journalists could not do their work. "My life has been profoundly changed since I was told by the government that I was on the extremist hit list," he said. "I'm not allowed to drive my own car. Everywhere I go, I have one man with a Sten gun sitting in the front, beside the driver, looking to the right, and another man sitting in the back with me, looking to the left. My driver has been given strict instructions not to allow any car to come near us. Since General Vaidya was assassinated, I have had to have a second car tailing me all the time, too. It sometimes seems to me that the only freedom we journalists can safely exercise now is the freedom to criticize the government." But, of course, all the security guards were government employees, and the government decided which journalists needed—or deserved—protection. It extended protection to the most influential journalists; some less influential journalists were murdered.

Until the Sikh extremists took up their guerrilla warfare, the only weapons that people ever carried were sticks. Subsequently, carrying guns and trafficking in guns became epidemic. People asked, "If the government cannot make the Hindus in Punjab safe in a preponderantly Hindu country, how can it protect other religious and ethnic minorities?" Not surprisingly, communities that did not yet have states of their own started wanting them. The latest group to agitate for statehood, the Gurkhas, would soon be asking for independence, it was said.

Ironically, Punjab was probably one of two states that, until the early nineteen-eighties, had made the most notable economic progress since Independence, and the other was Gujarat, which had had some of the worst outbreaks of Hindu-Muslim violence. Both states were now victims of a new urban class of educated unemployed, cut loose from the moorings of traditional village life on the land, who, with no work but with high economic expectations, were wheeling around towns and cities and attaching themselves to demagogic, fanatic religious leaders, as if they had found in religious ideals salvation from their economic plight. Indeed, events in Punjab revived the old fear that the country might fall apart and revert to an assortment of small warring nations, as in pre-Mogul times. One of the keenest observers of the Indian scene thought that if the Union was to be saved the country might have to fight an American-type civil war in Punjab. But he added that, since perhaps as much as a tenth of the Indian Army was made up of Sikhs, even if such a war could be fought and won it would only intensify the religious hatred.

Whatever Rajiv did he seemed to do in a hurry. Part of his hurry, no doubt, had to do with his not knowing how long he might live. Part of it may have had to do with the impatience of a young leader. (In the first two years of his rule, he changed the composition of his Cabinet eight times, with the result that before ministers could settle into their jobs and get to know their portfolios they were shifted to new positions or were out of office.) Part of it may also have had to do with his lack of political experience. In 1985, the Congress Indira Party, of which he was the president, celebrated its centenary. (Whichever party—Congress or Congress Indira—was in power always considered itself the inheritor of the original mantle.) A commemorative volume prepared and issued by the All-India Congress Committee created something of a scandal. On the cover it had pictures of Rajiv Gandhi's mother, grandfather, and great-grandfather, and many other Congress leaders, but, surprisingly, no picture of Mahatma Gandhi, the soul of the Party, the founding father of independent India, the man with whom the Indians' struggle for independence was most closely identified, and whom the poor most deeply venerated. Rajiv gave the opening address at the centennial celebration. Everyone in the Party expected him to pump up the Party workers with enthusiasm and pride. Instead, he attacked everyone, reserving some of his harshest words for the Party, and all but robbing the celebration of its festive spirit. He said at one point:

> As the proverb says, there can be no protection if the fence starts eating the crop. This is what has happened. The fence has started eating [the] crop. We have government servants who do not serve but oppress the poor and the helpless, police who do not uphold the law but shield the guilty, tax collectors who do not collect taxes but connive with those who cheat the

state, and whole legions whose only concern is their private welfare at the cost of society. They have no work ethic, no feeling for the public cause, no involvement in the future of the nation, no comprehension of national goals, no commitment to the values of modern India. They have only a grasping, mercenary outlook, devoid of competence, integrity, and commitment. . . . Instead of a party that fired the imagination of the masses throughout the length and breadth of India, we have shrunk, losing touch with the toiling millions. It is not a question of victories and defeats in elections. For a democratic party, victories and defeats are part of its continuing political existence. But what does matter is whether or not we work among the masses, whether or not we are in tune with their struggles, their hopes and aspirations. We are a party of social transformation, but in our preoccupation with governance we are drifting away from the people. Thereby, we have weakened ourselves and fallen prey to the ills that the loss of invigorating mass contact brings.

Millions of ordinary Congress workers throughout the country are full of enthusiasm for the Congress policies and programmes. But they are handicapped, for on their backs ride the brokers of power and influence, who dispense patronage to convert a mass movement into a feudal oligarchy. They are self-perpetuating cliques who thrive by invoking the slogans of caste and religion and by enmeshing the living body of the Congress in their net of avarice.

For such persons, the masses do not count. Their life style, their thinking—or lack of it—their self-aggrandisement, their corrupt ways, their linkages with the vested interests in society, and their sanctimonious posturing are wholly incompatible with work among the people. They are reducing the Congress organisation to a shell from which the spirit of service and sacrifice has been emptied. . . .

We talk of the high principles and lofty ideals needed to build a strong and prosperous India. But we obey no discipline, no rule, follow no principle of public morality, display no sense of social awareness, show no concern for the public weal. Corruption is not only tolerated but even regarded as the hallmark of leadership.

The government had been losing momentum. There was over-centralization in the Prime Minister's office, and Rajiv, for all his eloquence, didn't seem to know what his priorities were. Moreover, he was unable to restructure and revitalize the Congress Indira Party, or to make the civil service more efficient and responsive to his will—and the party in power and the bureaucracy were the country's two main instruments of government. Consequently, the early promise of his succession remained unfulfilled. Although he and the Congress Indira Party still enjoyed solid support in the country, he knew as well as anyone that if they were to stay in power they had to accelerate economic development. He was tilting toward a new economic course—one in which governmental controls were being relaxed as an incentive to the affluent entrepreneurial class. But the result was that he found himself trapped between giving entrepreneurs greater freedom to make money and keeping the loyalty of voters who were poor and whose situation was not going to improve, at least in the short term. Indeed, any economic benefits for the country at large would be a long time in coming. Meanwhile, he and his party had to face a general election, and the opposition was already taunting his regime as a government "by and for the rich." No characterization could be more politically damaging in a poor democracy.

Ever since Independence, India had functioned under a mixed economy, but with the public sector constantly encroaching on the domain of private enterprise. Then, in 1985, a wave of political conservatism, like that which had engulfed America and England in the eighties, seemed to be sweeping India. Vasant Sathe, the Minister of Energy at the time, wrote a series of articles for a national English-language daily in which he argued that the whole concept of the public sector—and, by extension, of socialism, which until Rajiv had guided government policies—might have been a mistake. The articles were seen as a sort of trial balloon sent up by the government, since it was assumed that one of Rajiv's ministers could not have voiced views contrary to the socialist policies of Rajiv's mother and grandfather without at least his tacit approval. Sathe's basic contention was that industry run by the government was inherently inefficient, because it attained high employment at the expense of productivity, and because the basic principle of efficiency was competition, which tended to be eliminated in the public sector. For instance, a hundred and twenty-five thousand workers in India produced less finished steel than fourteen thousand workers in South Korea. India produced finished steel for about six hundred and fifty dollars a ton, a very high cost when one considered the pool of cheap labor: per-capita income was two hundred and sixty dollars, in contrast to between ten thousand and fourteen thousand dollars in the developed countries. The domestic market for steel was limited in a poor country, and so India needed to sell its steel in the foreign market, but foreign companies found it much cheaper to buy Indian iron ore and make their own steel. Consequently, India earned only seventy-five rupees in foreign exchange for a ton of iron ore, when it could have earned four thousand rupees for a ton of finished steel. Furthermore, India produced only nine million tons of steel a year, when it could have produced many times that. And the production of steel could have provided huge direct and indirect employment, while the mining of iron ore could not do so. In colonial times, Indians complained that the British would take raw material out of India, create with it a finished product in their factories, give their own people employment, and sell the product back to Indians at a profit. Something similar was going on now, except that this time the Indians were doing it to themselves. The idea of socialism was to bring about the greatest good for the greatest number, but its effect had been to give rise to a whole new class of contractors and businessmen, who had grown rich on profits they made from government contracts.

Many people felt that Sathe's diatribe against the public sector and socialism was influenced by Reaganism and Thatcherism, and was simply dressing up Rajiv's predilection for private enterprise. They argued, for instance, that nowhere did he show why or how, under Indian conditions, private enterprise would be able to perform better than public enterprise, and said that even Rajiv's advisers acknowledged that socialism, whatever its bureaucratic or political failings, at least had an animating vision, whereas the idea of a free-enterprise system had only the vision of making more money. Whatever the rights and wrongs of the debate—and it was still at a very rudimentary stage—a consensus was forming in government and business circles that old socialist nostrums were no longer working. All the same, Rajiv's government could not dismantle the socialist structure, nor did it try to; it only opened up the country to more private enterprise than had existed before.

The people who stood to gain most from the new economic climate were a class of nouveaux riches who emerged in New Delhi, Bombay, and Calcutta. They had more money than any class of Indians had ever had before, and they behaved as if they saw themselves as a new "super" or "master" race. Self-confident, energetic, ambitious, and cosmopolitan, they could be at home anywhere in the world. Many of them were consultants, factory owners, builders, or contractors. Whatever they were, they did not work in the Indian subsidiaries of established international companies, in which, traditionally, people who couldn't get good jobs in government had tended to make their careers. Many of them were tax dodgers and black marketeers who contributed lavishly but surreptitiously to political campaigns and therefore enjoyed enormous influence in government and among politicians. Some of them talked as if they lacked the guilt of the rich people who came before them. In any case, they didn't see why they should feel any more guilty about the Indian poor than, for instance, the Americans or the British did, and they were apt to say things like "The Indian poor are not a national problem but a global problem." In conversation, they blamed the poor for remaining poor, and spoke of them as "extra human baggage" eating up the resources of the country without contributing anything to it. They said that if they were given free rein to invest and produce they would grow richer, and so would all the other people with entrepreneurial spirit, while the people who would go to the wall would have deserved to go to the wall. They held up the model of capitalism as it was practiced in Japan and South Korea, and brushed aside their critics, who said, for instance, that conditions in Japan were very different—that, unlike Japan, India could never become an export economy, because, given its huge population, it would always have enormous internal needs. B. K. Nehru, one of India's most distinguished civil servants, who had also served as Ambassador in Washington, High Commissioner in London, and governor of Jammu and Kashmir, explained in a lecture the newfound dominance of the class in this way: "During the Emergency, Sanjay traduced all the fragile institutions of our democracy—the civil service, the judiciary, the press, the civilian control of the military. He gave preference to this civil servant or that judge, intimidated this journalist or transferred that soldier. He therefore demoralized the whole apparatus of government. In his short life, he destroyed all the fragile democratic institutions that had been nurtured in independent India. Thus, he made possible the dawn of a totally ruthless, disillusioned period, where each man is for himself, for whatever he can get out of the society." There were no accurate statistics, but the number of these people was small. (Mostly because farm income was exempt from income tax, payers of income tax in the country were relatively few—numbering, perhaps, only three million—but, of course, there was no way of computing the number of tax dodgers.)

The emphasis of the earlier Congress leaders had been on improving conditions in the villages. Rajiv's emphasis seemed to be on the cities and towns, as if he believed that they were the engine of change, and believed in the trickle-down theory of economics— that in improving the lot of the urban middle class he would ultimately improve the lot of the village poor. Indeed, he was different from all his predecessors in that he was totally urban, with practically no experience in the rural regions of India. (One of his favorite slogans was "A computer in every village school by the twenty-first century." But a substantial number of schools in villages didn't yet have an adequate school building, a schoolteacher, a blackboard, chalk, or, for that matter, electricity.) The people who lived in the cities and towns included government servants, elected officials, doctors, lawyers, business executives, artists, journalists, shopkeepers, laborers, and those engaged in a hundred little trades. They were the people who had some purchasing power, some disposable income—who made up the consuming sector of society. They were responsible for the extraordinary growth of this sector since Independence. Indeed, the whole expansion of productive capacity in the public and private sectors had been geared mainly toward them. Thanks to them, India ranked ninth among the world's industrial nations in gross national product.

But the second India—village India—was where seventy-six per cent of the Indian people lived, and the way they lived caused the country to be ranked ninety-first among the nations of the world in per-capita income. Roughly five hundred and seventy million people lived in half a million villages. They continued to scratch out a livelihood as best they could as hired hands and small landholders, subject to the vagaries of monsoon and harvest. While here and there some rich people might have been found among them, most of them lived in a poverty unsurpassed in history.

Perhaps the most comprehensive account of poverty in rural India is the work of an Indian journalist, Kusum Nair. In a book entitled "Blossoms in the Dust: The Human Factor in Indian Development," which was published in London by Gerald Duckworth & Company, in 1961, she reported her observations of villages all across the country. About one in Uttar Pradesh she wrote:

> I went inside every single cottage in the village. They are small mud huts with tiled roofs. The entrance is very low and many have no doors. . . . [I]n none of the 85 homes is a *chula* [brick oven] alight or even with ash in it. In the corner near the chula are piled neatly, face downward, the cooking utensils,

earthen pots and a rare piece of brass. In one cottage there is a little cooked *sag* [spinach] in a pan, black in color.

The children—mostly naked, with hair matted and faces caked with dirt—stand around chewing on sticks of sugar cane and spitting out the remnants. The women are thin—their tattered sarees barely cover the body. . . . Holding me by the wrist, they take me into their homes, saying: "Come and see the tasteful dishes we have prepared for our mid-day meal," and lifting up their utensils they shake them upside down.

When I have been in all the 85 houses Hardwar Ram [an elderly villager] once again asks: "Do you believe us now? This is how it has been ever since I can remember."

Villages that had received special economic assistance from the government turned out to be no better off. Here Ms. Nair described the district of Mandya, in the south:

With the exception perhaps of a few individuals, the consumption of surplus income seems to begin and end with less personal work in the field and with the taking of coffee and better food in a hotel and going regularly to the cinema. According to a local estimate, nearly eighty per cent of these peasants in Mandya would still be in debt. Nor is the increase in their prosperity reflected in any other visible improvement in the manner and condition of their life. Everything else is as it always was, simply "because it has always been so."

Their houses have a small, square inner courtyard surrounded by a verandah, in at least three-quarters of which cattle are tied. In the remaining one-quarter of the verandah is the kitchen, and usually the latest arrival in a cloth cradle suspended from the roof, next to the cattle. The courtyard and the verandah are naturally filthy with urine and cowdung, and straw lies all around. . . . Even such peasants as have been persuaded in recent years to build a separate shed for cattle will still have half a dozen of their favourite animals inside the house, so that, according to them, they can look after them all the time and feed them at night. "We have always done it."

There is the superstition also that it is auspicious to see a cow first thing in the morning upon awakening. Despite all this love and reverence, however, the animals are of poor breed and emaciated.

Village lanes are generally full of stagnant pools and littered with straw, cowdung, goats, sheep, and bullock carts. Drains, where they do exist, made under schemes sponsored and subsidized by the Community Development administration, are green with scum and choked with dirt. Piles of rubbish, and even big boulders at times, lie undisturbed in the middle of some of the roads.

And although education is reportedly becoming highly popular in the district as a whole . . . [t]he usual early morning sight on the roads here is not of children going to school . . . but of barefooted children of six, eight, ten, collecting dry twigs for firewood and carrying small bundles of them on their heads or dragging them behind tied to a string.

I have regularly visited villages in different parts of the country since Ms. Nair published her account, and have found little or no improvement in the living conditions, as if "this is how it has been ever since I can remember" and "because it has always been so" were the sine qua non of a villager's existence. In any case, whatever economic strides have been made, their effect has been mostly vitiated by the huge jump in the country's population since Independence. (Officials say that so far science has not provided an effective birth-control method for a poor country; even Norplant is deemed too expensive. Nothing less than a vaccine or a draconian dictatorship will do.) India, by and large, has still to discover the benefits of modern plumbing, modern medicine, and modern social revolutions. And yet its defense budget has more than doubled in real terms over a period of ten or twelve years; it boasts the world's fourth-largest standing army; it has emerged as the Third World's top manufacturer of major weapons; it is the biggest importer of arms; and it has nuclear capability.

4

The Greatest
Factory-Based Accident

It is said that from the very beginning the Prime Ministership of
Rajiv Gandhi was dogged by bad luck—or, as many people in
India put it, was "ill-starred." When he had been in office only a
few weeks, the Indian newspapers were filled with reports on what
they all agreed in calling "the greatest factory-based accident in
human history." In the early morning on December 3, 1984, forty
thousand kilos of methyl-isocyanate gas was abruptly released into
the atmosphere by a pesticide plant situated in Bhopal, in the state
of Madhya Pradesh, in central India, and operated by the Indian
subsidiary of the Union Carbide Corporation. As white clouds of
the gas billowed from the plant, and the neighborhood and the
entire city misted over, people's eyes watered profusely, as if chili
powder had been thrown in their faces, and they gasped for air.
People vomited. People fell unconscious. People ran hither and
thither—some of them toward the plant—for cover. Many people
were crushed in the stampede. As a result of the accident, four
thousand people died, twenty thousand were injured, and five
million were exposed, in varying degrees, to MIC gas. There were
reports of survivors suffering, among other things, pulmonary tu-
berculosis, mental breakdowns, chromosomal changes, and repro-
ductive disorders. All the terrible aftereffects of the accident might
not be known for years. (According to one estimate, upward of two

hundred thousand people will continue to feel those effects far into the future.)

The explanation generally accepted in India for what caused the accident was that somehow water was introduced into the tank in which the MIC gas was stored, setting off a chemical reaction, and then protective mechanisms—one to neutralize the gas with caustic soda, another to burn it off—failed to function. At the time, most of the supervisory personnel had gone home. What the workers did or didn't do—or, for that matter, what they could have done—and a hundred other questions have never been answered.

Several civil cases, including one by the government of India, were filed against Union Carbide in different courts in the United States. Eventually, all the cases were consolidated and brought before Judge John Keenan, of the federal district court in New York City. The case, however, never reached the stage of dealing with substantive issues and their merits; it dealt only with the question of whether or not a United States court could have jurisdiction over the suit. In any event, no criminal charges were levelled against any American officials of Union Carbide, although when Warren Anderson, its chairman, flew to Bhopal to investigate the accident the government denied him access to the plant and its records, and arrested him, as if it intended to start a criminal proceeding against him. The Prime Minister's office intervened, however, and he was quickly released and flown home. The press continued to be filled with allegations of gross negligence at the plant. It was said that safety precautions were primitive, that workers often did not wear required gloves and breathing masks, and that as a consequence of false economies on the part of management the plant was understaffed, supervisory personnel were untrained, and some critical spare parts were unavailable. Some apologists for the company maintained in its defense that an accident like Bhopal could have occurred just as easily in an advanced country as in a poor, underdeveloped country; the examples of Three Mile Island, in the United States, and of the dioxin contamination in Seveso, Italy, were often cited. And then, on August 11, 1985, a toxic gas made up of several chemicals escaped from a Union Carbide plant in Institute, West Virginia, injuring at least a hundred and thirty-five residents of the area—this after a new safety system had been installed in the plant, in response to the accident in Bhopal. Yet the very fact that the Bhopal plant was in a poor country must have made it more accident-prone. Laborers in India have to work under the debilitating pressures of poor diet, poor health, poor housing, and poor wages, and often have a large number of children and relatives to support. They may have no easy means of transport to their place of work, and may have to travel long distances on foot to reach it, whatever the weather. Their efficiency and their attitude toward their jobs are bound to be very different from those of workers in an advanced country, living and functioning in a better-controlled and more orderly environment and in more healthful and more affluent circumstances.

When the Bhopal plant was constructed, in the nineteen-sixties, it was in a sparsely populated area of the city, and was simply a mixing and packaging plant. In the late nineteen-seventies, Union Carbide substantially expanded the plant and started producing the lethal methyl-isocyanate gas under a license from the central government, which had insisted that the gas, the raw material for the pesticide, be manufactured in India. (The government had long stressed domestic industry and economic self-reliance over foreign imports and dependence on other countries.) It has been argued in retrospect that the company would have been well advised to move the plant to an area outside the city limits, where other industries considered hazardous were situated; and, in fact, in 1975 the state legislature had passed a comprehensive town-planning act for Bhopal which stipulated that there should be no hazardous industry within the city. The state town-planning department later labelled eighteen industries hazardous or "obnoxious," and started monitoring them, but the list did not include the pesticide industry, possibly because it was essential to domestic agriculture. Consequently, Union Carbide was exempted from rules that applied to other industries producing hazardous materials in the state, and so kept the Congress Indira state government in the good graces of a rich American company. (Politicians often got jobs at the plant for their relatives and friends.) Meanwhile, slum settlements had grown up around the plant. A few of the squatters had casual employment in it, but most of them were tonga drivers, cigarette sellers, bicycle repairmen, milkmen, porters, sweepers—poor people such as inevitably settle around any industrial plant in India and piece together a livelihood by providing services for its employees. In April of 1984, Arjun Singh, the chief minister of the state, had given the squatters around the plant ownership of the bits of land under their makeshift shacks and lean-tos, and so legalized what had been illegal settlements. His motive may have been either to win votes for the Congress Indira or to help the poorest of the poor. Whatever it was, the change made the dangerous situation worse. Around that time, a minister was specifically asked in the legislative assembly about the the site of the Union Carbide plant, and his reply was that it was "not a toy to be played around with." Someone else in the assembly observed that the plant represented an investment of two hundred and fifty million rupees. (At the time, the rate of exchange was twelve rupees to the dollar.)

After the accident, some Indian lawyers argued that the state government—because it did not clear away the settlements or carefully monitor the hazard that the plant posed to the community—should share the responsibility for its severity, and therefore the victims or the victims' families should sue not only the Union Carbide Corporation but also the state government. Other lawyers pointed out that, even if the state government was culpable, a common-law principle known as sovereign immunity would block the use of the courts—themselves part of the government—to sue the government. Anyway, the target of all the court cases seemed to be the corporation. After the accident, many American lawyers rushed to India, got themselves Indian law partners, went to Bhopal, and signed up, on contingency, large numbers of the injured and the families of the dead for individual lawsuits, to be tried in American courts against Union Carbide. These lawyers aroused public hostility, and in March, 1985, the Indian Parliament passed the Bhopal Act, which gave the central government sole authority to represent the victims. The Indian partners of the American lawyers challenged the constitutionality of this act in a written petition presented to the Indian Supreme Court, on the ground that if the Court should decide in favor of the Indian government there would still be a problem with the government's speaking for the victims, since if it was a guilty party it could not, in good conscience, arrogate to itself the right to speak for those whom it injured. There was also the separate issue of whether an American court would agree to assume jurisdiction over the case when the accident occurred in a country some ten thousand miles away and much of the evidence and many of the witnesses were there. Still, it was pointed out in India, the designers of the plant and the top officials of the corporation were Americans, and were in the United States. Lawyers in India discussed two contradictory precedents in which an American company was involved in an accident in a foreign country. One concerned the crash of a Piper airplane in Scotland; in that instance, the Supreme Court decided, in July, 1976, that the United States was not the proper country in which to try the case. The other concerned the crash of an Air India Boeing 747 in Bombay in 1978, after which the families of the victims sued the Boeing Corporation in the state of Washington; in that instance, a federal district court allowed the case to be tried in the American courts. Dr. Armin Rosencranz, the executive director of a California-based non-profit organization called the Pioneer Fund, who had made a study of the legal and environmental aspects of the Bhopal accident, concluded that the United States court might do well to ask the Indian courts to deal with the Union Carbide case. Many people in India hoped that the lawsuit or lawsuits would be decided in the United States, because the monetary value placed on lives lost and injuries sustained was hundreds of times that placed on them in India. The Indian Workmen's Compensation Act fixed at ten thousand rupees, or about eight hundred and thirty-three dollars, the liability of a company for a life lost on the job because of proved company negligence, except for extraordinary cases, in which it allowed for forty thousand rupees. In any event, the slum dwellers would not have been covered by workmen's compensation, because they were not employees; they were a "third party" in the eyes of the law. What was more to the point, however, was that it was not clear from the evidence available how employees other than those working in the plant at the time of the accident could claim coverage. But then most Indian workmen's-compensation cases never go to court. Litigation in India is so protracted and Kafkaesque that people seldom turn to the courts for remedial action.

It was often pointed out in India that the victims of the Bhopal accident who had died were beyond the reach of compensation. But soon it appeared that their families and the injured might also be beyond the reach of compensation. Most of the survivors were casual laborers. Many of them never had a postal address. Many of them had the same first name, or similar first names, and no surname. They were never enrolled on the register of any company—had no employment record of any kind. Moreover, by the time the lawyers were discussing the question of venue most of the survivors of the accident had probably drifted off, to the villages from which they came, or to any spot where they could find casual work, or to any spot where they could get their stomachs filled. It was soon being said in India that, whatever the eventual award or settlement, whether it reflected American largesse or Indian scantiness, the only money the survivors themselves would ever see would be what the state government had distributed within days of the accident, apparently with an eye to the general election that was to be held a couple of weeks later, in mid-December—the election in which both the month-old Prime Ministership of Rajiv and the future of the state government were at stake. The state government had then given ten thousand rupees to every family that could prove that a close relative had died, two thousand rupees to every victim "seriously affected," and a thousand rupees to every victim "not so seriously affected." Thereafter, people in India thought that the compensation case would probably be settled out of court.

Whatever the outcome might be, people in India took it for granted that pesticides would continue to be produced in India. The country's next Five-Year Plan called for doubling their production. Pesticides were necessary to raise crop yields and to keep the nation's much-needed foreign exchange from being spent on the importation of foodstuffs. In fact, there was no means of getting away from the production of huge quantities of pesticides if Indians were to be fed and were also to be saved from the ravages of parasite-borne diseases like malaria and filariasis, still endemic in Southeast Asia.

In February, 1989, more than four years after the accident, the parent Union Carbide Corporation and Rajiv's government reached an agreement under which the former was required to pay to the Indian Supreme Court a total of four hundred and seventy million dollars in settlement of all outstanding claims. The agreement was challenged in the Indian Supreme Court as inadequate, under a procedure that permits a petition for "review" of the Court's judgment—the settlement was about one-seventh of what had been asked in a civil suit filed by Rajiv's government itself in 1986—and Rajiv was bitterly attacked for "selling out" to American business interests. While the judicial review was taking its tortuous course (a decision from the Supreme Court was handed down only in October, 1993, when it dismissed the petition), politicians were reported to be busy doctoring the lists of claimants—substituting names of friends and political workers for those of the poor, illiterate families of many injured and dead—so that when the money was finally doled out it could line the pockets of the politicians' supporters.

The money was not released until October of 1992. By that time, the claimants had come to number about six hundred and fifty thousand, of whom fourteen thousand had asked for compensation related to deaths. The victims' relatives sometimes had to make the rounds of seventeen courts in order to establish the genuineness of their compensation claims, and that December, on the eighth anniversary of the accident, the government's welfare commissioner stated that out of a total of nine hundred and ninety-five compensation claims for death five hundred and ninety-nine had been thrown out, because the next of kin could not "conclusively prove" that death had occurred.

5

The Divorced
Muslim Woman

Early in 1978, in the town of Indore, in Madhya Pradesh, an indigent, illiterate Muslim woman, Shah Bano Begum, filed a claim with the local magistrate against her husband, Mohammed Ahmed Khan, who, she said, had thrown her out of their house. Her application demanded that her husband provide her with a living-maintenance allowance, as Indian law required. She was about sixty-two years old, had been married to Mohammed Ahmed Khan for about forty-six years, and had borne him five children. Then, in November, in the course of the legal controversy between them, her husband announced that he was divorcing her. Subsequently, he contended that since Shah Bano was no longer his wife the courts had no jurisdiction in the matter—that as a divorced woman she was entitled to a maintenance allowance for only three months, as Muslim personal law prescribed. (According to the same law, to effect the divorce he was required to do nothing more than to pronounce the words "I divorce you" three times.) In August, 1979, however, the magistrate decided in favor of Shah Bano, and ordered Mohammed Ahmed Khan to pay her a monthly living-maintenance allowance of twenty-five rupees, or about two dollars. Shah Bano appealed the amount of the award, and eventually the high court of the state raised it to a hundred and seventy-nine rupees and twenty pice, or about fifteen dollars at the time. (What the formula was for arriving at this odd figure is presumably known only to legal scholars.) Although Mohammed Ahmed Khan was a lawyer and was earning perhaps as much as five thousand rupees a month, he refused to pay, and appealed the decision to the Supreme Court. In April, 1985, the Court, in the case of Mohammed Ahmed Khan v. Shah Bano Begum and others, ruled in favor of Shah Bano, holding that divorced Muslim women, like other Indian women, were entitled to maintenance. The judges based their opinion primarily on the Criminal Procedure Code of 1898—more specifically, on the code as it had been revised in 1973—and, as the revised code specified, they set the maximum maintenance a husband would have to pay at five hundred rupees a month, and made payment of any amount conditional on the wife's having no other means of support and on her husband's having sufficient means to pay it. Even so, the opinion touched off a huge religious and political controversy: Were Muslims to be governed by the secular laws of modern India or by the canonical laws of their ancient religion, which were based on Allah's commandments and on words and deeds of Muhammad, and of which Muslim personal law was a part? (In theory, at least, the canonical laws were supposed to govern all the political, economic, civil, criminal, ethical, social, and domestic affairs of Muslims.) In other words, were Muslims Indians first or Muslims first?

Muslim clerics, leaders of Muslim organizations, and fundamentalist Muslim politicians attacked the decision as meddling in Muslim personal law, and accused the judges of setting themselves up as interpreters of Islam. The Supreme Court judges had buttressed their arguments with references to the Koran, to Islamic canonical law, and to a host of Islamic scholars, and now apologists for the Supreme Court pointed out that the defendant's side was the one that had first introduced the religious arguments, and that the judges had only responded to them—but this rebuttal was in vain. Some Muslim liberals hailed the decision as a step toward bringing Muslim women into the modern world, but even some of those liberals seemed to speak from both sides of their mouths. For example, Agha Fazal, a lawyer who tried cases before the Supreme Court, said, "If maintenance is against the . . . Islamic laws, let our women not ask for it. But if they go to court, then the court is bound to go by the law of the land." G. M. Banatwala, the general secretary of the Indian Union Muslim League, put forward a private member's bill in Parliament to amend the Criminal Procedure Code so as to deny maintenance to divorced Muslim women. In 1973, when Parliament drafted the revisions to the code, there had been such an outcry from Muslims about a provision giving the courts the right to issue orders for the maintenance of all divorced women that Prime Minister Indira Gandhi's government had added a second—contradictory—provision, to the effect that the courts, in granting maintenance, should first consider whether the woman was receiving the amount due to her from her husband under whatever religious personal law applied to the parties involved. (The provision did not address the question of what would happen if she was.) The contradiction had bedevilled subsequent legal disputes, but in a series of judgments beginning in 1974 the courts had resolved it in favor of a provision giving maintenance to all divorced women. In the Shah Bano case, the Supreme Court was only reaffirming what the courts had held. The Banatwala bill was intended specifically to bar the courts from granting maintenance to Muslim women, and to insure that Muslim women had no right to claim maintenance beyond the prescribed three months.

The influential journalist Arun Shourie reported in the *Times of India* that in August of 1985—about four months after the Supreme Court's ruling—Arif Muhammad Khan, a Muslim and a junior minister, ran into Rajiv at a reception and told him that he would like to speak on the Banatwala bill. Rajiv said no, because Khan would only be repeating what other proponents of the bill would be saying. Arif Muhammad Khan said that, on the contrary, he wanted to speak against the bill, because he was convinced that asking a husband to support an indigent divorced woman was in accord with the spirit of the Koran and Islamic canonical law. Rajiv walked away to talk to other guests but later returned and said that he approved the idea of Khan's speaking on the bill, and Khan, it seemed, interpreted this to mean that Rajiv's government would oppose the bill.

Shourie, whose account was apparently based on what Arif Muhammad Khan had told him, followed up the story. When, a couple of weeks later, Khan made his speech on the floor of Parliament, he received a letter of congratulation from Rajiv himself. Subsequently, Rajiv praised him in the Cabinet, saying that one could find many liberals in the Muslim community but seldom did one come across a man of such courage. Shortly afterward, however, it became clear that in the state of Assam, where an election was to be held in December, Congress Indira candidates were losing Muslim support, partly because of the Shah Bano judgment, and also because of an accord that Rajiv had signed with Assamese student leaders which was intended to disfranchise or expel all the predominantly Muslim refugees who had been pouring into the state from East Pakistan—and then from Bangladesh—since 1961. (The refugees who had come before 1961 were deemed to be Assamese.) In the middle of the Assam campaign, another junior minister, Z. R. Ansari, made a speech in Parliament denouncing the Shah Bano judgment and the Supreme Court as well. Arif Muhammad Khan evidently felt that the speech could have been made only with Rajiv's approval, and that the rug had been pulled out from under him. He had second thoughts when, later, he was told that Rajiv had personally substituted his name for that of another minister to accompany Rajiv on a trip he was making to Oman. (Indian politics had acquired all the trappings of a royal court.) And in the course of the trip Khan was led to believe that Ansari's speech was only a bit of campaign propaganda for consumption in Assam. But then, in the December election, Congress Indira was routed.

All along, Muslim leaders had been spreading the word that the Shah Bano judgment made every Muslim in the Indian Union insecure. In one city, nearly a hundred thousand Muslims demonstrated against the judgment. In another city, a mob of ten thousand Muslims stoned some fellow-Muslims who advocated religious reform. Here, the All-India Muslim Personal Law Board announced plans to set up religious courts; there, other Muslim organizations met to plan their strategy. The atmosphere became so highly charged that Shah Bano herself petitioned the Supreme Court to rescind the judgment. Rajiv was shaken. Muslim voters had been one of his family's most dependable constituencies during its more than thirty years of ruling India. At one point, before the Assam election, Rajiv asked four prominent journalists, including Shourie, to meet privately with him and his ministers to discuss the Banatwala bill. In describing the meeting to me, Shourie said, "The ministers were telling Rajiv in front of us that in India religious law had always been sacrosanct—the government had never interfered with the practices of the personal law of any religion. Rajiv seemed to believe them. I said, 'Sir, your ministers are lying to you. They are bowing to political expediency. The British never hesitated to interfere with religious law when it conflicted with their civil or criminal law.' I cited Lord William Bentinck's famous abolition of suttee in 1829. I quoted other examples, going back a hundred years, and mentioned the fact that Muslim criminal law had been replaced by the Indian Penal Code, of 1860, to say nothing of the Criminal Procedure Code. I told Rajiv that Hindu practices had been similarly curtailed, by laws like the Caste Disabilities Removal Act, of 1850. I brought up acts like the Married Women's Property Act, of 1874, which, one by one, had extended the reach of the modern, secular state. The ministers looked very embarrassed. Their faces got red, and Rajiv didn't seem to know what to do or say. But it was clear to me that Rajiv had succumbed to the hysteria whipped up by Muslim fundamentalists and to fear of the consequences of losing the vote in Assam. I came away feeling that he was well meaning but didn't have the experience or the background to deal with the duplicitous ministers. Nor did he have a lot of advisers. As far as anyone knows, he's had only two close advisers, Arun Nehru and Arun Singh, and one is a cousin and the other a school chum."

In late February of 1986, Rajiv's government introduced the

Muslim Women's bill, which dealt with protection of divorced women's rights, and which superseded the Banatwala bill. It put the responsibility for supporting indigent divorced women not on their husbands but on their parents and other relatives, and on *wakfs,* or Muslim charitable trusts. In introducing the bill, the Law Minister said that it had consistently been government policy to defer to the leaders of a community in matters pertaining to its interests. Arif Muhammad Khan immediately sent in his resignation. Arun Singh, Arun Nehru, and Rajiv, in turn, tried to prevail upon him to retract it, for the sake of Party unity, but he refused, feeling that the bill was inimical both to the progressive elements of his religion and to the secular principles of the Party and the country; indeed, he felt that the bill put India behind many Muslim countries, which had been modernizing Muslim personal law.

Rajiv's Muslim Women's bill, which became law in May, was seen as a terrible blunder all around. For example, even the Muslims dismissed as impractical the idea of *wakfs'* supporting indigent divorced women. In the Muslim tradition, a believer can create a *wakf* for charitable purposes, but he can retain its profits for his own subsistence and for the subsistence of his descendants and relatives as long as his family line continues. Although there are perhaps a hundred thousand *wakfs* in India, and each state has a governmental *wakf* board to oversee those within its boundaries, the system has been so grossly misused that in 1976 a governmental commission looking into it reported, "With the lowering of the general standards of morality and integrity in all sections of society, the increasing tempo of materialism, and dilution of spiritual values, the number of black sheep among the [*wakf* managers] has naturally grown enormously during the past few decades." (Soon afterward, many of the same Muslims who were saying that the government shouldn't meddle with Muslim personal law were clamoring for the government to clean up the *wakfs* and the *wakf* boards.)

The passage of the Muslim Women's bill turned a civil issue into explosive material for religious strife. There were signs everywhere of a Hindu backlash against the bill, of anti-Muslim feeling, and of a resurgence of Hindu extremism, whose adherents sought to turn the secular Indian state into an out-and-out Hindu state. Nehru, Rajiv's own grandfather, was responsible for the Hindu Code bills, which in the nineteen-fifties reformed many of the old Hindu practices. For instance, Hindus had discriminated against women, but the constitution guaranteed equal rights for men and women. In one of the bills—which was intensely resisted by Hindu traditionalists—Hindu daughters, who had been barred from inheriting ancestral property, were put on an equal footing with Hindu sons in matters of inheritance. The fact that Hindu practices were reformed despite widespread Hindu opposition had since colored Hindu attitudes toward Muslim personal law. Some Hindu extremists had charged all along that behind the defense of Muslim personal law was a Muslim scheme to encourage the practice of polygamy and produce more children, in order to raise the proportion of Muslims in the country. Ominously, the Muslim Women's bill might have given a signal to the Sikhs that they could fight for a Sikh personal law. It was said that Rajiv might have set the stage for the eventual destruction of the secular state, which his grandfather and his mother had labored so mightily to guard and nurture. But then they had lived much of their lives under the shadow of the Partition and had been haunted by the threat of religious war. At the time of the Partition, Rajiv was just three years old.

6

The Telephone Exchange Caper

One summer day in 1985—a year after Operation Blue Star—the ringing of the telephone in our hotel room in New Delhi jolted me out of a deep sleep. I answered, only half awake.

"There is a fire in the hotel, and we need some information to plan an evacuation," a man's voice said in my ear.

"A fire? Where is it?" I asked.

"So far, it is confined to the basement, but all the elevators are shut down. What is your name? . . . How many are in the room? . . . Are there any children?"

I dutifully gave the answers, telling the caller that I had with me my wife and our baby daughter.

"Is your wife wearing a nightie?"

"Why?"

"Is it of polyester? If so, please ask her to immediately change into a cotton nightie."

Even as I was talking on the phone, a waiter wheeled in the breakfast that we had ordered the night before, and set it up. My wife drew back the curtains and said something about swimmers playing in the pool ten floors below.

"Wait a minute!" I said into the phone, sitting up. "If there's a fire, how can you be serving breakfast?"

"Please, get your wife to change her nightie immediately."
There was a loud disconnect.

I was fully awake, and I called the reception desk downstairs
and asked about the fire and the strange call.

"Fire? There is no fire. It must be a telephone hoax."

I knew from my visits to India over the years that some kind of
danger always lurked around the corner. One minute, a back street
would be as peaceful as a mangy street cow eating from a dustbin in
the sun, and the next minute a shouting mob would materialize,
like the wasps one sees swarming around the hotel doors in the
morning. Before one knew it, knives would be flashing and Mo-
lotov cocktails flying. I myself took seriously any warning of danger in India, and I asked the receptionist if hotel guests often
received alarmist telephone calls.

"I would not like to say, sir, please," the receptionist said.

For the rest of the morning, there were telephone calls and
emissaries from the lobby manager's office, from hotel security,
from the hotel's public-relations office, all bent upon assuring us
that we were as safe in the hotel as we would be in our beds in
America. The fuss was out of proportion to its cause—the silly
telephone call—but then, I reminded myself, the hotel had a
vested interest in keeping its guests in ignorance of the dangers
within and without: of the fact that we were in the capital of a
smoldering country with the brushfires of factional strife starting
up now in a city here, now in a village there. Our hotel was one of
half a dozen five-star hotels in New Delhi, with perfect air-
conditioning and good water pressure, modern plumbing and
modern fixtures—Western comforts out of the reach of almost all
the people living in India. The hotels were built during Prime
Minister Indira Gandhi's regime, to attract foreign tourists and
foreign conventioneers, foreign exchange and foreign business, and
they allowed one to be in India without requiring one to cope with
any of its realities. (One night in our hotel, without meals, cost us a
hundred dollars, or six months' wages for an average Indian. Ordi-

narily, I would have felt too guilty to go near the place, but this time I was travelling with a small child.)

The day after the telephone hoax, I woke up to newspapers with these banner headlines: "NORTH INDIA ROCKED BY BOMB EXPLOSIONS!" and "40 DIE IN BLASTS IN DELHI, U.P. & HARYANA." The front page of the *Times of India* carried, in bold type, this summary of the night of bombings: "Sikh terrorists struck in different cities and towns of Northern India today, leaving about 42 dead and more than 100 injured in a series of well-planned and organised bomb explosions in buses, trains, and crowded localities. The new feature of the renewed outbreak of terrorist activity is the planting of explosives in crowded buses in a bid to create a fear psychosis and immobilise people." Later newspaper reports raised the number of deaths to eighty, and stated that many of the victims were children: one little Hindu boy found a transistor radio in the street and took it home, only to have it explode in his hands, killing him and his whole family.

One hot summer evening a year later, during another visit, as my wife and I were getting ready to go to bed in our hotel room in New Delhi the telephone rang. I picked it up. There was no one at the other end. I put it down, and it immediately rang again. I picked it up, but again there was no one there. Whenever I visit India, I thought, my life gets taken over by the telephone. Our daughter, whom my wife was nursing on the bed, started to cry. The telephone rang repeatedly, but no one ever seemed to be at the other end. I suddenly became aware that there was a continuous ringing of telephones all around—in the hall outside and in the adjacent rooms. I removed our telephone from its cradle and tried to ignore the ringing elsewhere. It occurred to me that the continuous ringing might be the hotel switchboard's sophisticated way of announcing that it was out of order. Our telephone certainly looked high tech; besides the regular touch-tone buttons, it had an extra set, labelled A, B, C, and D.

My wife, who had quieted the baby, began looking through the directory of hotel services for a number to call to report the telephone problem. There seemed to be a number for practically anything anyone would want—Beer, Breakfast, Churches, Doctor, Drinking Water, Electricity, Hospitality, Ice, Lost & Found, Packed Lunches & Dinners, Photographer, Safe-Deposit Lockers, Sewing Kit, Shoeshine Service—but there was nothing for Telephone Repair. Then she read out this bit from the directory: "Please bear with us for a not-too-efficient Delhi city telephone service. All international calls are routed through Bombay, so connecting your call may take some time."

Eventually, the telephones stopped ringing, and we were able to go to sleep. During our stay in New Delhi, the hotel telephones kept starting to ring of their own accord every so often. The hotel management blamed the Indian telephone equipment for this. We found the ringing unsettling, rather as the old people in Muriel Spark's novel "Memento Mori" get rattled by an anonymous caller who rings them up at all hours and says, "Remember you must die." By coincidence, we were soon exposed to another telephone drama, this one enacted on a national scale.

On August 22, 1986, the front pages of the national dailies carried such headlines as "P. C. SETHI GOES BERSERK" and "PHONE STRIKE AS SETHI 'ABUSES' OPERATORS." The Sethi episode quickly came to dominate not only the news but also casual conversation, since it gave people a new excuse to attack the political establishment, the telephone service, and the Army. It seemed, from the newspaper accounts, that on August 21st, at 11:05 P.M., an "urgent" telephone call, which has priority over pending "ordinary" calls, was placed to Bombay from New Delhi as a "V.I.P. booking," which has priority over other "urgent" calls. It was booked from the government residence of Prakash Chand Sethi, a member of Parliament for the ruling Congress Indira Party and a former Minister of Home Affairs—one of the three or four most important government positions in the country. The night operator who handled the call said she had reported back that there was no reply at the Bombay number. She said she had tried the call again five minutes later, as is customary with "urgent V.I.P. bookings," and had again reported back that there was no reply. A few minutes later, a new, "lightning" call, which has priority over all "urgent" calls, was placed, also as a "V.I.P. booking," from the Sethi residence to the same Bombay number. The night operator said that when she called back a third time to say that there was still no reply she spoke to Sethi himself. It seemed that Sethi didn't believe that she had ever tried to place his call. According to her, he told her that he was coming down to the telephone exchange to "settle scores" with her; abused her in obscene language; and said he knew that girls like her could be had for five rupees, as if to say that she was cheaper than the cost of his call to Bombay. "I was hurt at what he was saying," the operator later told the Delhi *Sunday Mail.* "But what could I do? After all, it was a V.I.P. booking."

At around one-thirty in the morning, Sethi, who was sixty-six years old and the father of six children, arrived at the Delhi central telephone exchange carrying an automatic pistol. He was accompanied by one of his sons-in-law and by two bodyguards armed with Sten guns. He forced his way past the security staff, stormed up to the ninth floor, where the night operators work, roundly abused all and sundry, and confronted the operator who had handled his call. "Mr. Sethi . . . abused me in front of my colleagues," the operator told the *Statesman.* "He was dead drunk and blew the smoke from his cigar at my face several times. He also brandished a pistol and threatened that he would kidnap me. When some of my colleagues came to my rescue he lay flat on the floor pretending to be innocent." Around the same time, he apparently got into a scuffle with a male supervisor and with another man, who had summoned the police. There was pandemonium at the exchange.

The women operators jumped up onto the tables and squatted there, shouting for Sethi's arrest. The telephone workers called for a strike.

When the police arrived, they found Sethi lying on the floor with his pistol beside him, and they apparently carried him out of the building. In due course, three formal charges were lodged against him: assault to deter a public servant from performing his duty; trespassing in order to commit an offense punishable with imprisonment; and insult with intent to provoke a breach of the peace. He was not, however, arrested. It was immediately said that the charges were pro forma—that because of his high position nothing would ever come of them. In any event, Sethi gave the press a totally different account of what had happened.

According to Sethi, he had been trying to get through to a relative in Bombay for at least two and a half hours before the time reported in the newspapers, and he claimed that it was impossible that the Bombay relative would not have answered the ring, since that person must have been at home and his telephone was by his pillow. It was in order to examine the various reference tickets for his call—to establish for himself that the operator had not done what she said she'd done—that he had gone down to the exchange, he said. He explained that he was carrying a pistol and had armed bodyguards with him only because government regulations advised such precautions for people who were on a Sikh extremists' hit list, as he claimed to be. At the exchange, he had been set upon by the women operators. "It was they who abused me," he told the press. "These women formed a ring around me. I was pushed by their union secretary. I even fell down." He told the *Sunday Mail* that at no point had he been drunk or had he abused the night operators, adding, "If I wanted to . . . misbehave with women I know where I have to go. I wouldn't wander into a restricted area"—a reference to the exchange. He told the *Statesman,* "I have not talked to [the] Prime Minister's house about this. Why should I bother him with this?" He all but threatened to dismiss the police commissioner and his deputy in the event that he became Home Affairs Minister again, and he charged that "the whole episode has been manipulated to malign me in public." Indeed, in the press accounts he sounded unrepentant, saying that the operators were "fat, lazy ladies, every single one of them." (The fact is that for years now there has been direct dialling between Delhi and Bombay, so Sethi could have avoided going through the operator altogether, but then he would have got no priority; no one knows whether he might have been able to get his call through.)

Sethi was not without his sympathizers. On the heels of his escapade, the *Indian Express* published an account of one New Delhi subscriber's frustrating experience with Indian telephones. One evening, at around six o'clock, he found that his telephone had gone dead. He cursed, and called Complaints from a neighbor's house. The operator noted down his number and his address, and gave him a "ticket number." At nine-thirty the next morning, his telephone was still dead. He called Complaints again, and was given three different numbers at which to try to reach the supervisor. He got no reply when he called the first two numbers but did reach the supervisor at the third. The supervisor said that he would remind the repairmen. At 1:30 P.M., the telephone was still dead. The subscriber tried the three numbers for the supervisor again, but this time he got no reply from any of them. When he did eventually get through to one of the numbers, he had to give all the particulars to the supervisor once more. On this occasion, however, the subscriber pretended to be a high city official. The repairmen came immediately, traced the trouble to a squirrel's having chewed through wires in the junction box, and got his telephone working. The moral of the story seemed to be that if the subscriber had not used the ruse about his identity he might have been without a telephone not for twenty hours or so but for days.

"Why blame Mr. P. C. Sethi?" another telephone subscriber, this one from Calcutta, wrote to the *Telegraph.* "How many of your readers will swear, hand on heart, that they are not inclined to do the same to every telephone department functionary, minister downwards? It's just that it takes a former Union Home Minister to throw circumspection to the winds and act." And the New Delhi correspondent for the London *Times,* Michael Hamlyn, wrote in his paper, "Anyone who has dealt with the women of the central exchange will have a sneaking sympathy for Mr. P. C. Sethi." He went on to explain to his readers, "Communications are one of the most frustrating aspects of living and working in India. . . . The attitude of the exchange staff does not help. It is often off-hand, uncomprehending, and mulish. Horror stories abound, and many subscribers have felt like taking a pistol down to the exchange and sorting them out."

A friend of mine in Delhi used to say, "Telephones here look like the real thing until one tries to use them." Often, one found it impossible to get a dial tone. If one did get it, the telephone might ring busy at the dialling of just the first digit of the number. It was so difficult to complete a call that some offices employed people whose only job was to keep dialling numbers. If one did succeed in completing a call, it might be only to reach a wrong number. If one reached the right number, telephone conversation might be drowned out by cross-talk or bursts of static, or the telephone might simply go dead. During the heavy monsoon rains, telephones in whole areas remained out of commission for days. And there were other anomalies. Overseas calls were routed (by operators) through the Indian space satellite, but local calls relied on equipment that was in some cases at least fifty years old. Consequently, a call to London might be put through within a couple of hours, but a call to Bombay might take a couple of days. Both the telephone service and the production of telephone equipment were in the public sector, and, although the government tried to modernize the system, its attempts mostly misfired. (In the seventies, it bought new switching equipment, but by the time the equipment was installed it was outmoded.) The government also tried to loosen its hold on the system by issuing licenses to local private manufacturers and by holding talks with foreign delegations interested in supplying materials to the Indian telephone industry. But these efforts, too, bogged down—in disputes over how much telephone equipment should be imported, and how much of the manufacturing of equipment in India should be turned over to private enterprise. On top of everything else, the telephone bureaucracy was notorious for being cumbersome, for widespread absenteeism, and for corruption. Bribes were routinely paid to get a telephone repaired; without official priority, it generally took five years to get a telephone and telephone connection. The government committed itself to spending three billion two hundred million dollars between 1986 and 1990 to upgrade the system, but the funds seemed not to be enough even to maintain it. The truth was that in the country's scale of priorities telephones had to be near the bottom. At the time, there were three million telephones in the entire country and a million would-be subscribers on the waiting list, and the people with telephones, of course, were the people with power and money. But they constituted less than half of one per cent of the country's population. Fortunately, however, in the nineteen-nineties there has been a marked improvement in the telephone exchanges of some major cities.

Whatever the state of the telephone system as a whole, and whatever the truth about Sethi's particular experience with it, on the day of his escapade the workers at the exchange, who included three thousand women, wrecked some of the telephone equipment, went out on strike, and picketed the exchange, cutting New Delhi off from the rest of the country and from the rest of the world. They demanded Sethi's arrest and also better security and better working conditions. Leaders of the opposition parties and of organizations like the All India Democratic Women's Association expressed solidarity with the strikers and clamored for a high-level inquiry into the whole episode.

Sethi's escapade embarrassed the ruling party and the government of Rajiv Gandhi. Sethi had been a loyal Congress politician, holding important posts almost continuously since 1962, in the governments of Prime Ministers Nehru, Lal Bahadur Shastri, and Mrs. Gandhi. (Sethi was one of the few ministers in her Cabinet whom Rajiv had not appointed to a high office when he succeeded his mother.) He had sat in Parliament for a total of twenty-one years, and in addition to his job as Minister of Home Affairs he had held such Cabinet portfolios as Minister of Chemicals and Fertilizers, Minister of Works and Housing and Petroleum and Chemicals, Minister of Railways, and Minister of Planning and Irrigation. He had also been the chief minister of his home state of Madhya Pradesh for nearly four years. To save face after the exchange escapade, Rajiv's government followed a policy toward the strikers which combined intimidation and appeasement. It surrounded the exchange with troops and police, tried to restore a modicum of service with the help of operators from the Army's Corps of Signals, and threatened the workers with dismissal. At one point, the police charged the pickets. Around the same time, the Minister of State for Communications, R. N. Mirdha, met with deputations of strikers and listened to their grievances. Mirdha also made public a letter of apology from Sethi, in which Sethi said that he had been worried about a personal problem and had been distraught at not being able to reach his relative in Bombay; that, in his anxiety, he had gone to the exchange to try to get his call through; but that he had had no intention of insulting or injuring the telephone staff, and was sorry that some "sisters" had felt "hurt" because of his behavior. After three or four days, the strike was broken, amid widespread complaints that the use of the Army at the exchange was yet another example of the government's resorting to military force to settle what were essentially social and political problems. (The spectre of a military coup haunts all poor countries. Political observers in India, though, maintain that the Indian Army is made up of too many diverse groups and interests to organize a coup, and that the country is too large to succumb to military rule.)

In the meantime, Sethi had repudiated the letter of apology almost as soon as it was made public. An emissary from Mirdha,

Mr. Bhajan Lal, had visited him in the middle of the night and "had brought a draft of [the] letter to Mr. Mirdha supposed to [have been] written by me," Sethi told the press. "I made some changes in the draft, and started writing it out by hand, as there is no typist in my house at night. Mr. Bhajan Lal said he would get the letter typed by someone else, so I put my signature on my blank letterhead on the understanding that my revised draft would be typed on it." He said that in the revised version he had not admitted having done anything wrong at the exchange (and hadn't made any such admission in the original version, either) but had merely expressed the hope that the troops surrounding the building would be withdrawn, that the strikers would return to work, and that telephone subscribers' "suffering" would be ended.

Sethi's statement about the preparation of the letter, like his account of events on the night of his call to Bombay, was received with considerable skepticism by the press. It was noted, for instance, that he was under doctors' care for depression, and also that his escapade at the exchange was but the latest example of increasingly erratic behavior on his part. The day before it took place, he had visited Chandigarh, and while staying at the official guesthouse he had made a public spectacle of himself by standing on the balcony in his underwear in the middle of the night and berating the staff for not providing him with adequate security. Before that, at the festivities at the Red Fort on Independence Day, August 15th, he had shouted at some security people because he wasn't allowed to sit in the front row, which was reserved for "Very, Very Important Persons," and later that day he had created a similar rumpus at the President's house, first by taking a ten-year-old grandniece along to a reception to which children were not invited, and then by getting into an argument with Rajiv when the Prime Minister chastised him for his behavior at the Red Fort.

Many of the Congress Indira Party leaders dismissed Sethi's doings as isolated examples of aberrant behavior by an attention-hungry political has-been. But his rough-and-ready style was characteristic of Indian politicians. It sometimes seemed that all too many of the people who survived in politics—as in many other areas of Indian life—were blustering, aggressive, corrupt types, people who trampled on the rights of others. Every day during our visits, it seemed, there were reports of politicians engaging in outrageous behavior and sexual harassment. In 1986, for instance, the capital was buzzing with the latest revelations about J. B. Patnaik, who had been the chief minister of the state of Orissa since 1980. A cover story in *The Illustrated Weekly of India,* a leading English-language magazine, datelined May 18–24 and headed "SHOCKING! THE STRANGE ESCAPADES OF J. B. PATNAIK," detailed the politician's alleged "nepotism," "corruption," and "systematic sexual exploitation of vulnerable men and women." In newspapers and in drawing rooms, Patnaik's doings were a lively topic of conversation.

Around the same time, a story in the *Times of India* about a women's conference in New Delhi read:

> The incident involving Mr. P. C. Sethi is only the symptom of a malaise which has gripped the higher echelons of society. People in high places, with their money and power, treat human beings as their property and debase the dignity of women especially. . . . Women belonging to multifarious organizations expressed anguish at the fact that in spite of his "indefensible" behaviour, Mr. Sethi had not been arrested. Another disturbing trend was that mostly in the cases involving assault on the dignity of women, political leaders holding high offices were involved and in spite of exposures of their misbehaviour no action was taken by the higher ups, they said. . . .
>
> The meeting also deplored the activities of the chief minister of Orissa, who reportedly exploited women sexually. The speakers demanded the immediate resignation of Mr. Patnaik.
>
> The fact that the Prime Minister had not issued any statement so far on the conduct of Mr. Sethi invited the ire of all women present. It only meant his silent approval, they said.

Women's organizations were by no means alone in deploring immorality in high places. The travails of the Indian political establishment may well be only a reflection of the problems of contemporary India, in which a patina of modernity overlies what is essentially a medieval society.

7

Rajiv's Perestroika

In the summer of 1988, during a visit to New Delhi, I noticed signs everywhere of the emerging "modern India," as people like to call it. Not long before, television had been a novelty available to few, and television programs little more than amateurish radio newscasts with pictures. But that year it was estimated that between fifty and seventy million people watched two ambitious television series, and also a historical drama about the Partition of India. That was close to the estimated number of consumers in India with some disposable income, and the demand for everything had so outstripped the supply that for most goods there were government lists of numbers and priorities. By Western standards, consumers in India lived very modestly, but their increasing numbers were a testament to India's high rate of economic growth in the seventies and eighties.

The monsoon had failed in 1987, and as a result the country had suffered one of its worst droughts in a hundred years. In the fifties and sixties, even a less severe drought could have led to near-famine conditions. In such a case, the government would have been forced to spend its scarce foreign exchange on foreign foodstuffs. There would no doubt have been pleas for foreign aid. But the coming of the green revolution in the seventies—the construction of dams and canals, the electrification of villages, the drilling of wells, and the improvement in seed strains, fertilizers, storage facilities, transportation, and distribution networks—meant that, while there were food shortages, high inflation, and seething discontent, there was no famine. This seems nothing less than a miracle in the light of India's population growth. The drought created a severe water shortage almost everywhere. In the middle of the drought, the water from the Yamuna River, one of the main sources of Delhi's supply, was diverted by the neighboring state of Haryana to farms within its boundaries, worsening the effects of the drought upon the capital. Many neighborhoods didn't have water for more than three or four hours a day, and even when they did have it the water pressure was inadequate. (In the desert state of Rajasthan, only a hundred miles to the west, women were walking as far as five miles each day in the hot sun and waiting in line for hours to get a bucket of water.) To supplement the municipal water supply, many affluent people were forced to drill wells, but, because the water table had dropped, the wells had to be drilled ever deeper. The government was reduced to taking out pathetic advertisements in newspapers contending that New Delhi had first claim on the country's water. "CAPITAL'S HISTORIC CLAIM" was the head on one such advertisement, and the text read:

> It is no accident that civilization first dawned along the banks of the Tigris and Euphrates, or that the civilizations of Egypt and India developed in the valleys of the Nile and Indus. . . . Delhi is situated and has grown on the banks of the Yamuna. So, according to all conventions, Delhi would have the top priority to get raw water from the river. But it is the last to get it. Delhi keeps on persuading the neighbouring States for raw water. It is overlooked by the States that the city of Delhi was older than all the irrigation systems encircling it. . . . Delhi as the National Capital belongs to the country. It is, therefore, the moral obligation of all the States to look after its well-being. Particularly, the neighbouring States should stand by the Capital in its need for water which is crucial to human life. Their coöperation will be appreciated by lakhs

[hundreds of thousands] of people. . . . In Delhi, enough flow is not always available in the river Yamuna to run the existing Water Treatment Plants. . . . Delhi's requirements of water supply should [be] given priority over demands of water for irrigation purposes. . . . To be fair to Delhi, the neighbouring States of Haryana and Uttar Pradesh should provide additional raw water to Delhi to meet its minimum requirements of potable water. If you have any suggestions to strengthen Delhi's case for more water please send them to:

Jag Parvesh Chandra
Chief Executive Councillor
Delhi Administration,
Old Secretariat, Delhi

In the past, most state governments were under the control of the ruling Congress Party, and the central government simply ordered them to do its bidding. At the time of the drought, however, many states were under opposition governments, and these took every opportunity to embarrass New Delhi. So the advertisements only publicized the impotence of the central government and the spreading fear in the capital that if the monsoon were to fail in 1988, too, its people and the country would be ravaged by famine and disease. It happened that the monsoon rains in 1988 were plentiful. (As is often the case, they caused fatal floods in some parts of the country.) But the drought awakened people to the realization that since Independence there had been something wrong with the whole system of national priorities, under which, year after year, the government devoted a major portion of its budget to defense—including, some speculated, the building of an atomic bomb—while failing to meet age-old needs for clean air, safe drinking water, and the disposal of human waste. It was being said that the great strides of modern India in industry and agriculture had been made at the expense of the basic requirements of the people.

Because the capital served as the showcase for the country's progress, more attention and money, as a matter of course, were spent on meeting these elementary needs there than in most of the other cities. Indeed, once upon a time people in New Delhi took pride in their healthful drinking water, and derided foreign visitors for boiling the water even to brush their teeth. They joked about "Delhi belly," mild temporary stomach upsets that people got occasionally, and boasted about how much better off they were than people living in Calcutta, say, who had to drink water sometimes infected with sewage, and consequently suffered from chronic amoebic dysentery and a variety of mysterious fevers and viruses. Since the early eighties, though, the drinking water in Delhi had threatened to become almost as undependable as that in Calcutta. And in 1987, certainly, a lot of Delhi residents were afflicted with chronic dysentery and other illnesses. There was also an epidemic of cholera that year—something previously unheard of in New Delhi—and people who could boil their drinking water were doing so even in the relatively disease-free winter months. The water shortage continued up to the monsoons of the following year, and had the additional effect of exacerbating the perennial problem of the disposal of human waste—the main source of disease. As had long been the case in Calcutta, people who were fortunate enough to have the convenience of toilets complained that there was no water to flush them; the nearby railway tracks, which most poor people used as latrines, seemed to be cleaned even less frequently than in the past. And, because of the combination of the growth in population, increased road traffic, the use of outmoded vehicles, a boom in construction, and the installation of an electric-power station, the air in New Delhi was choked with soot, grit, and dust.

As usual, one was struck by how cheerful and resilient both the rich and the poor were. The support system of family, servants, government jobs, and a growing economy seemed to keep people going. But the city as a whole seemed rundown, discouraged, and sickly. And the situation in other Indian cities, not to mention villages, was worse. It was as if Calcutta were a sign of the country's future.

Rajiv's Perestroika

When I was in India in 1985, Indians, who like to seek refuge from their miserable reality in what they see as the glamour of everything foreign, were comparing their newly elected Prime Minister, Rajiv Gandhi, with the newly chosen General Secretary of the Soviet Union, Mikhail Gorbachev. It was said that, like Gorbachev, Rajiv understood that he could coast along if he accepted the political and economic system he had inherited, but that, also like Gorbachev, he believed that the good of the country required him to open the economy to free enterprise, introduce a modern, streamlined management style, democratize and revitalize the ruling party (in Rajiv's case, the Congress Indira Party), and clean up corruption—that is, attack his country's basic political and economic problems, whatever the personal or political cost. Indeed, the term *perestroika* was sometimes used for Rajiv's new political and economic order. Within months, however, people were rarely mentioning Rajiv in the same breath as Gorbachev, and they began telling this fable about Rajiv's *perestroika:*

A fox looks up and sees a crow flying backward. "Brother, why are you flying backward?" he asks. "Haven't you heard about *perestroika?*" the crow replies. "Everyone must go backward to capitalism in order to get ahead in socialism—that's the new order." The fox thereupon runs backward straight into a bear, and the bear mauls him and chews off one of his legs. The fox says to the crow, "Brother, why are you still flying backward? Look at what happened to me." The crow says, "Haven't you heard, brother? *Perestroika* is only for the upper echelons."

Early in 1986, the *Indian Express* published articles alleging that the chairman of Reliance Industries, Dhirubhai Ambani, who was a business titan and was thought to be a major contributor to the Congress Indira Party, had imported machinery illegally, and Rajiv's government had looked the other way. The articles clearly implied that, as always, money could buy off the government. Ambani was locked in corporate warfare with another business titan—Nusli Wadia, the chairman of Bombay Dyeing. And Wadia was a friend of Ramnath Goenka, the rich owner of the *Indian Express*. The articles were dismissed by some as a plant by Wadia to embarrass Ambani, but a financial adviser to the *Indian Express*, S. Gurumurthy, wouldn't let the story die; he claimed to have many documents substantiating the allegations. In any event, in October of 1986 the Finance Minister, Vishwanath Pratap Singh, quietly authorized the Fairfax Group, a private American management-consultant firm specializing in detective work, to look into the allegations. V. P. Singh's action was bold, unprecedented, and politically hazardous, for any involvement of an American agency in Indian affairs was bound to raise the spectre of the Central Intelligence Agency, which had been a scapegoat in Indian politics for a long time, and especially since its well-publicized role in overthrowing Prince Sihanouk in Cambodia, in 1970, and President Allende in Chile, in 1973.

In January of 1987, V. P. Singh's authorization of the Fairfax investigation became known, whereupon Rajiv, who had not been consulted about it, abruptly transferred him out of the Finance Ministry, and what the Fairfax Group had uncovered was not divulged. Getting V. P. Singh out of the Finance Ministry may have been only an expression of Rajiv's pique that Singh hadn't talked to him before involving a foreign agency in Indian affairs. Or it may have been an example of what Indian newspapers called Rajiv's increasingly immature, erratic behavior; a couple of days earlier, he had all but dismissed the Secretary of External Affairs during a press conference. Whatever it was, it started a damaging rumor that Fairfax had unearthed evidence of payments—kickbacks—to government agents by foreign companies for securing them defense contracts; that some of these kickbacks had been paid to the actor

Amitabh Bachchan, who was famous for his roles in countless popular films as an anti-establishment Angry Young Man; and that, in violation of Indian foreign-currency rules, Amitabh's kickbacks had been stashed in secret Swiss bank accounts by his brother Ajitabh Bachchan, who had taken up residence in Switzerland the previous year. Amitabh Bachchan had long been one of the closest friends of the Gandhi-Nehru family, and, as a result, in the general election of 1984 he had easily won election to a safe Congress Indira seat from Allahabad, the family's home town. At the time of Singh's exit from the Finance Ministry, Rajiv was not only Prime Minister but also Defense Minister, and a rumor began circulating that Amitabh Bachchan was keeping some of the money for Rajiv, and that Singh had kept Rajiv in the dark about Fairfax because Rajiv himself was under investigation. Singh, for his part, maintained that his authorization of the Fairfax investigation was within the mandate from Rajiv to root out corruption wherever it existed. In any case, the impression that Rajiv was shielding his friends became popularly accepted.

On the heels of Singh's exit, Girilal Jain, the editor of the *Times of India,* which was one of the country's most pro-government English-language dailies, published a biting signed editorial attacking Rajiv for seeing himself not as first among equals but as "king-emperor." Jain thought that Rajiv exercised wider powers, and exercised them more easily, than either Gorbachev or Deng Xiaoping, and that his being able to do so betokened a grave weakness in the Indian democratic system. The editorial was one of many lambasting Rajiv.

A couple of months earlier, during the *Indian Express* and Reliance Industries controversy, Parliament, despite outcry from the press, had passed what was called the Indian Postal Act (Amendment) bill. It allowed the government to intercept and open private mail. The avowed purpose of the bill was to stem the tide of terrorist activities, the Sikh separatist movement in Punjab having rapidly become more violent. In January of 1987, the President of India, Zail Singh, refused to sign the bill, on the ground that it violated the fundamental constitutional rights of Indian citizens. Earlier, as Home Affairs Minister in Mrs. Gandhi's Cabinet, Zail Singh had actually supported the introduction of the bill, so the assumption was that at this time he was trying to take advantage of Rajiv's political troubles and score political points at his expense.

Since, in contrast to previous Presidents, Zail Singh was essentially a small-time local Punjabi politician, many of Mrs. Gandhi's followers had little use for him. They contended that Zail Singh had been ineffective as the Congress Party chief minister of Punjab and that when, in 1977, he lost out to the Akali Dal he had encouraged a rival fundamentalist Sikh movement—the movement that ultimately spiralled out of control and led to the Sikh occupation of the Golden Temple. Although Zail Singh had supported Mrs. Gandhi's Operation Blue Star, he had gone to the temple immediately afterward to do penance for it, thus giving the impression of running with the hare and hunting with the hounds. It had never been any secret that Zail Singh viewed Rajiv, who was almost half his age, as a spoon-fed baby with no other claim to the Prime Ministership than that he was his mother's son. But Rajiv was the intended successor of his mother, and after he was nominated as Prime Minister by the bigwigs of her party Zail Singh had no recourse but to swear him in. It was said that Rajiv, in the first seven or eight months of his Prime Ministership, shut Zail Singh out of many official proceedings, most notably those concerning a subject in which, merely as a Sikh, Zail Singh could be deemed to have a natural interest. That subject was the four-day riots in New Delhi following Mrs. Gandhi's assassination. In 1986, a commission of inquiry headed by a Supreme Court justice, M. P. Thakkar, published a report on the riots which clearly corroborated the widespread assumption that Hindu Congress Indira politicians had abetted, and even staged, some of them, to avenge Mrs. Gandhi's death and the killings of Hindus by Sikhs in Punjab; people already knew that the Hindu police had stood idly by during the riots, thus becoming accomplices. Zail Singh was said to feel that he had later been barred by Rajiv from official information and deliberations of the Cabinet, to which, as President, he had a right. Though a figurehead, he was the Commander-in-Chief, and he had some residual powers, as the monarch does in the British parliamentary system, on which the Indian system is modelled. For instance, if two people had competing claims for the office of Prime Minister and it seemed that either could win a vote of confidence in Parliament, the President could choose one over the other and force Parliament to vote on his choice. There was, however, no tradition of regular contact between the President and the Prime Minister in India, as there is in the comparable British system: in Britain, the Prime Minister formally calls on the monarch every week for an "audience." Nevertheless, since Indian Presidents, by and large, had been venerable national figures, previous Prime Ministers had generally kept them informed, out of respect for both their persons and their office. Zail Singh believed that he was being discriminated against because he was a Sikh; and, indeed, observers said that Rajiv had gratuitously provoked a row with him over the President's prerogatives. The result was that Zail Singh became a dangerous rallying point for the opposition parties and for Congress dissidents as a series of corruption scandals broke over Rajiv's head, the Fairfax scandal being the first.

On March 9, 1987, less than two months after V. P. Singh's exit from the Finance Ministry, Zail Singh wrote what he called a "private" letter to Rajiv. "The president/prime minister relationship in our country is governed by certain well-established practices and conventions besides express provisions of the Indian constitution," he wrote, and he went on to assert that in the previous two years those conventions had not been followed, so he could not determine whether Rajiv was conducting the government in accordance with the letter and the spirit of the constitution. He seemed to be making their personal differences a constitutional issue and, at the same time, putting in doubt the constitutionality of Rajiv's conduct of his office. In order to insure that his letter would have the maximum public effect, he apparently leaked it to the *Indian Express,* for on March 13th it was splashed on the front page.

For some time, Arun Shourie, who was then the second-in-command of the *Indian Express,* and was also its conscience, had been the scourge of the government, and the government saw the publication of the letter as the final provocation. Immediately, the Central Bureau of Investigation, which generally deals with serious crimes, raided the house of the paper's owner, Ramnath Goenka. The Bureau accompanied its raid, which turned up nothing, with the arrest of S. Gurumurthy, the *Indian Express's* financial adviser, who had doggedly pursued the Fairfax affair, and with a search of the paper's offices and the seizure of several supposedly incriminating documents, which were said to reveal illegalities having to do with the building in which the paper was housed and with the paper's imported printing presses. By the government's own admission, the supposed violations had occurred over several years, so few could doubt that the timing and manner of the raid and the arrest, search, and seizure had more to do with political revenge than with any illegalities. The Bureau's action, which kept the *Indian Express* from publishing its Delhi edition for a hundred and seventeen days, was seen as a bungled attempt to muzzle the press (the Bombay and other editions continued to appear as usual), and seemed to confirm growing popular suspicions that Rajiv was seeking to cover up corruption in his government.

Rajiv's crippling rows with the President and the press coincided with campaigns for midterm elections for legislative assemblies in three key states, separated from one another by at least a thousand miles: West Bengal, Kerala, and Jammu and Kashmir. Since the general election of 1985, Rajiv had lost state elections in three other states—Karnataka, Punjab, and Assam—so it appeared that his popularity was falling precipitously and his name, the Congress Indira's biggest asset, was losing its lustre. As usual, the 1987 state elections were fought on local issues, but Rajiv seemed bent on turning them into a national referendum on his stewardship of the country. For instance, in West Bengal, where a Communist, Jyoti Basu, was standing for a third term, Rajiv campaigned personally—something that no Prime Minister had ever previously done in any state—thereby putting the prestige of his office on the line. The elections were held on March 23rd, and the Congress Indira was all but routed. In West Bengal, it suffered an unprecedented third straight defeat, and it also lost Kerala, to a Communist-led coalition. Only in Jammu and Kashmir did it have a measure of success.

On removing V. P. Singh from the Finance Ministry, in January, Rajiv had made him Defense Minister. In the middle of February, almost before Singh had settled into his new job, a report was brought to his notice that a huge kickback had been paid for the government's contract to buy four submarines from a West German company, Howaldtswerke Deutsche Werft. The contract had been negotiated in 1980, while Mrs. Gandhi was Prime Minister. Around that time, she had ruled that all middlemen were to be dispensed with in the giving out of defense contracts, and that where the practice of paying a commission—a euphemism for "kickback"—to middlemen was standard the amount of the commission was to be deducted from the price that the government paid for the contract. Then, in 1983, she had formally authorized the contract for the four submarines, at a cost of three hundred million dollars. It was subsequently reported within the inner circles of the Defense Ministry that seven per cent of that sum, or twenty-one million dollars, had been paid to an Indian agent for the contract, the payment being made in installments between 1980 and 1987. And Rajiv had served as Defense Minister from October, 1984, through January, 1987. In Indian terms, the amount of the kickback was so large that it dwarfed previous scandals. It was generally believed that no private citizen could have taken the money and kept it for himself, and so it had to have been given either to the Congress Indira Party or to the Gandhi family. In any case, for six weeks V. P. Singh did nothing about the report, which had the potential to besmirch the reputation not only of Rajiv and the Congress Indira Party but also of Rajiv's late mother. Then, on April 2nd, just after Rajiv's authority had been challenged by Zail Singh, Michael Hershman, the president of the Fairfax Group, gave a tantalizing interview to the *Statesman,* in which he said that V. P. Singh's removal as Finance Minister had come immediately after Fairfax informed the government that a "key witness" was about to give significant evidence of kickbacks. The witness, Hershman said, had subsequently refused to testify. But Hershman was now on public record as all but saying that Singh's removal was part of Rajiv's coverup. Rajiv responded by removing several of Singh's colleagues, then still at the Finance Ministry, who had shared the responsibility for the Fairfax investigation, and replacing them with loyal new officials—an action that naturally caused newspapers and opposition leaders to charge that he was brazenly continuing the coverup. At the same time, he appointed M. P. Thakkar and another Supreme Court justice, S. Natarajan, to sit as a commission of inquiry on the Fairfax affair, charging them, however, to look into the conduct not of the government but of V. P. Singh and his colleagues. The Thakkar Commission, as it came to be called, was seen as an attempt to make sure that the scandal would not be examined closely but, rather, would be contained and whitewashed. Both Thakkar and Natarajan were known to feel great reverence for Mrs. Gandhi. A few days after the appointment of the commission, V. P. Singh launched an inquiry of his own into the kickback allegations, without telling Rajiv. Immediately, the nature of the allegations somehow got into the press, and Singh had no choice but to quit—he resigned as Defense Minister and left the Cabinet on April 12th—since he knew that he no longer enjoyed Rajiv's confidence. The upshot was that Singh became a martyr overnight, not only in India but in the world at large. The London *Times* noted that Singh's "personal incorruptibility made him stand out in a field crowded with racketeers." Closer to home, the *Indian Express* stated in an editorial on its front page, "No Prime Minister has confirmed the worst allegations and suspicions about his probity as Mr. Rajiv Gandhi has." The editorial went on to say that V. P. Singh could not possibly have embarrassed Rajiv with his German-submarine inquiry unless Rajiv "or someone dear to him" had taken a kickback. The editorial was one among many indications that Rajiv's reputation had, as people like to say in India, "fallen to the bottom of the sea."

On April 16th, Rajiv sat impassively in Parliament while members of the opposition parties denounced his government as "steeped in corruption." (Three days later, the officer who had been appointed to take charge of the four West German submarines upon their delivery shot himself, only increasing the sordidness of the scandal.) Also on April 16th, the Swedish national radio came out with a charge that in 1986 the Bofors unit of Nobel Industries Sweden AB, the largest arms manufacturer in Sweden, had agreed to pay kickbacks to senior Indian politicians and defense personnel to secure a contract for field guns, and had already paid a total of nearly five million dollars into an account, code-named Lotus, at the Schweizisher Bankverein, in Geneva. Negotiations for the Bofors field guns had begun in 1977—again, under Mrs. Gandhi. The contract, which had been authorized by Rajiv in 1986—again, when he was Defense Minister—was for the purchase of four hundred towed howitzers at a cost of one and a third billion dollars, and, when the story broke, it was said by the newspapers that he had promoted the Bofors claim for its field gun over claims for field guns built in other countries. The Bofors scandal was perhaps the most unsavory in the history of corruption in independent India.

For the rest of April and during all of May, there was a flurry of statements by both the Indian and the Swedish governments and by Bofors, all denying that any kickbacks had been paid, but few gave the statements any credence. It was taken for granted that the two governments would try to protect each other, in order to maintain trade and good relations, and that Bofors would try to shield the Indian officials it had paid kickbacks to, in the hope of doing future business with them. On one occasion, in April, Rajiv, his senior Cabinet colleagues, the state chief ministers of the Congress Indira, and other Party leaders met and passed a Party resolution that all but accused the United States and Pakistan of touching off the scandals in order to imperil Indian national security and thereby destabilize Indian democracy. A month later, Rajiv all but accused the United States of complicity in the assassination of his mother as well, saying at a Congress Indira rally in New Delhi, "Indira Gandhi was killed because she fought against imperialism and because she made India strong and independent. I vowed to continue her fight and today we are in open confrontation with the same forces who destroyed her." The speech was an echo of speeches that his mother used to make about the "foreign hand" whenever her government was beset by scandals or other deep political troubles: she would accuse the United States or the C.I.A. of working to destabilize Indian democracy in order to create chaos and replace her socialist government with a right-wing, pro-Western, capitalist government. The strategy had had the effect of unifying factions behind her, but now, under Rajiv, it didn't work. At one point, Rajiv came up with the alibi that he had discussed the Bofors contract with Sweden's Prime Minister, Olof Palme, and that Palme had assured him there would be no kickbacks. Since Palme was dead, that statement couldn't be corroborated, so the attempted alibi only weakened Rajiv's standing further.

The Indian opposition and the press carried the day, and finally, at the end of April, the Swedish government directed Sweden's National Audit Bureau to launch an investigation. It did not get very far, however, because Bofors, after making a show of coöperation, stonewalled. All the same, in June the bureau issued a report. Some of its sections were classified, but its conclusion was made public; namely, that an agreement between Rajiv's government and Bofors for the payment of commissions to middlemen had existed, and that the company had incurred a cost in paying those commissions. Thereupon, in parallel actions, Rajiv sent a mission to Switzerland, purportedly to try to find out the identity of the holder or holders of any secret bank accounts, and the Swedish government appointed a public prosecutor to investigate the affair. But nothing came of either of these moves, and perhaps nothing could have: Rajiv's government was investigating itself, and, besides, in Parliament it could easily dominate the opposition; and the Swedish public prosecutor could not establish a prima-facie case against close-mouthed Bofors. At any time, Rajiv could have cleared everything up by simply demanding that Bofors make public the names of the people to whom it had paid kickbacks—a demand that the company could hardly have ignored, since Rajiv retained the power to cancel its field-gun contract. Consequently, the belief took hold that Rajiv had something to hide—that his friends, at least, had "eaten money." (Food metaphors are commonly used in India, perhaps because staving off hunger is still the preoccupation of most of its people.) This belief was strengthened by a second interview that Hershman gave to the *Statesman,* two months after the Fairfax Group was dismissed; in the interview he charged that at the time of the dismissal the investigation was about to confirm large-scale corruption in Rajiv's government, and that the appointment of the Thakkar Commission was "part of a cover-up being perpetrated by Mr. Gandhi." Hershman also stated that he knew of a number of American firms doing business with India which had paid a "contribution" of five per cent of the value of their pending contracts to "offshore welfare funds." (In 1986, the International Monetary Fund had estimated that private Indian deposits in Swiss banks exceeded a billion dollars.)

A few days later, Rajiv made a solemn categorical statement in Parliament that neither he nor any member of his family had received any consideration in the Bofors deal. Certainly there was no hard evidence that Rajiv had ever had his hand in the till, and even the circumstantial evidence implicating him was extremely thin. Many thoughtful people in India believed that either he had been taken for a ride or he had shown excessive loyalty to his friends.

But the Thakkar Commission's report, when it was issued, in February, 1988, only heightened the storm. It stated, for instance, that any inquiry into the activities of economic offenders—that is, purveyors of "black money," or money off the books—should be undertaken only by the Cabinet collectively, with the knowledge and sanction of the Prime Minister. The report noted:

> The leaders of the world would not conduct their affairs vis-a-vis leaders under a cloud with the requisite degree of trust and confidence which are essential for arriving at a mutually advantageous long term relationship. The voice of such a handicapped country with such a handicapped leadership would become weak or inaudible or would not carry the same weight or inspire the same faith. The long term relationship in the spheres of trade, commerce, and industry would be prejudicially affected. It is therefore a specious argument that destabilising the leader of the party or the leadership in charge of the administration at a given point of time, will not result in destabilising the country. Such a situation could certainly result in great detriment to the national interest and national security.

Critics like Arun Shourie were quick to pounce on this passage, saying that it must have cheered the purveyors of black money, since a widespread government discussion of their activities would be bound to have many leaks, tipping them off, and, at the same time, would tie the hands of any independent investigator.

In the early years of Independence, there was a certain idealism animating government socialist policies in India, and, for the most part, corruption was kept in check. For instance, during Jawaharlal Nehru's seventeen years as the country's first Prime Minister the ruling Congress Party generally solicited contributions in an open manner from businessmen and private individuals—anyone who could afford to give. The solicitations were considered a legitimate

Party function, and contributions were made mainly by check and were recorded and accounted for.

A big change took place after Indira Gandhi became Prime Minister. In her government, a feeling grew that officials, to be really socialist and left-wing, should not be under obligation to business in any way. Contributions from big business to political parties were therefore banned. But elections became more and more expensive to wage and harder and harder to win, so politicians needed more and more money. They began accepting it from businessmen in cash, quietly, under the table. This black money often required the use of all kinds of middlemen, and they took their cuts or kickbacks along the way, because no accounts were kept of what money was paid out, or to whom.

Another big change took place in 1975, when Sanjay became an important force in the government. He saw to it that the kickbacks routinely made by overseas companies to get contracts were no longer made to middlemen; instead, the kickbacks were made directly to his minions or to Congress Indira Party functionaries—and that came to the same thing. Mrs. Gandhi's minister would wear his official hat during contract negotiations with representatives of a company, and then, on agreeing to award it a contract, would put on his Congress Party hat and add, "Provided you give *x* amount of money to my party." Kickbacks, sometimes of as much as ten per cent, were automatically collected from foreign companies on most contracts negotiated by, among others, the Defense Ministry, the government's largest spender. Sanjay's rationale was: Why should any money be siphoned off to middlemen when he and his party could have it all to themselves? Some of the money collected was laundered and used for election purposes, but the suspicion was that a good deal of it was salted away in undeclared foreign bank accounts, especially in Switzerland. Politicians used the money for all sorts of private purposes, it was said—to take foreign holidays, to buy foreign education for their children, to build a nest egg. A sort of symbiotic relationship developed between politicians and businessmen—businessmen at home and abroad. Politicians facilitated the doing of business by granting businessmen licenses and favors, and by overlooking their infractions of various government regulations. The favors and the infractions grew right along with socialist rhetoric and socialist legislation, and businessmen filled the Party coffers. The system of kickbacks quickly became so deeply entrenched that after Sanjay's death Mrs. Gandhi's ministers justified it as a necessity for fighting and winning elections—for keeping India democratic. It seemed that there was no governmental or party activity that was not tainted with black money; and, indeed, a "black economy," or black market, had developed alongside the "white economy." Everyone in the political sphere, from the most important minister to the least important functionary, was on the take, or so it was popularly believed. The discussion was never about the principle of accepting kickbacks; instead, it was about the size of particular officials' take. No one questioned, for instance, the unfair advantage that the party in power gained by collecting money for its candidates. In fact, to be in Indian politics and remain incorruptible seemed an impossibility, like squaring the circle. And people in business started talking about kickbacks "in terms of loot instead of corruption," Girilal Jain wrote.

Still another big change took place in 1984, with the accession of Rajiv and his stated policy of cleaning up the government, which was apparently the fruit of a sincere wish. Party leaders had chosen him in the first instance not because he was one of them but because he was the heir of the Nehru-Gandhi family and therefore offered the best hope of their continuing in office. Once he had consolidated his power, however, he barred all payment of commissions to agents of foreign arms suppliers and let it be known that, since socialist nostrums had proved ineffective, he intended to liberalize the socialist system of government licenses and controls, eliminating the need for any greasing of official palms. As if to back his words with action, he appointed V. P. Singh his Finance Minister, making him the most powerful person next to the Prime Minister himself.

V. P. Singh was imbued with Mahatma Gandhi's concern for the poor, and was zealous in the pursuit of his principles. Moreover, although he had been chief minister of the state of Uttar Pradesh and Minister of Commerce in the central government, he was not a powerful figure in Congress Party politics, and that meant he had no political debts to pay, no claims of a personal or national constituency to satisfy. He set about the task of liberalizing the economy and reforming the budget, seemingly without giving a thought to the consequences for himself. He all but declared war on the business community, ordering police raids on the Delhi residences of some of the most illustrious names in Indian industry, his aim being to uncover evidence of tax evasion, of illegal foreign bank accounts, or of the importing of goods without proper licenses—of black money. In the past, such police raids, which were attended by shaming publicity, had been conducted against notorious black marketeers and big-time film stars but not against top industrialists, who were often major behind-the-scenes contributors to political parties. In fact, the only precedent for Singh's raids was the dreaded police raids that Sanjay had masterminded during the Emergency, but the object of those raids had been to bully businessmen into contributing money to the Congress Party instead of to opposition parties. Singh seemed to want to make an example of his victims and to reform the business community. He was soon being spoken of as a Savonarola, who would burn down Florence rather than allow sin to prosper. The terrorized industrialists appealed to Rajiv, who, as the president of the Congress Indira Party, was indirectly responsible for raising money for it. But his victory had decimated the opposition parties, and he seemed to bask in the glory that the raids reflected on him.

The Party's need for money couldn't be put off indefinitely, however, and after a few months in office Rajiv started accepting contributions. A charitable view is that Rajiv himself didn't take kickbacks but relied for Party funds on people who were new and untrained, unworldly about the collection of money and about kickbacks. If so, those people bungled. As a consequence, the Party may have succeeded in collecting more money, but Rajiv couldn't distance himself from the collection process, as his mother had; she had always relied on professionals, three or four steps removed from her. One heard that under Rajiv, therefore, fewer people along the way could take kickbacks, and, for all anyone knew, that situation may have stirred up a certain resentment against him and made him vulnerable to charges of personal corruption. Some people said that he never tried to clean up corruption—that the whole purpose of his much-heralded modern management style was to prevent leaks about kickbacks, and that anyway such a style was suited only to running an airline company, never to running a vast country. However that may be, he could no longer count on his original constituency, which had given him his big victory, and so, ironically, he was thrown back on the very Congress machinery of bosses and intimidation from which he had seemingly tried to dissociate himself, but with this difference: in dealing with the Party machinery, he was in a much weaker position than his mother had ever been. True, the entire process of collecting money was murky, and most of what was reported about it was hearsay. What was incontrovertible was that there seemed to be no way of diminishing the role of black money in politics short of instituting state funding of elections. But that issue had scarcely been raised. And it could be said that democracy itself bred corruption, in the sense that parties needed war chests and businessmen needed favors.

The convergence of the overlapping scandals and the emergence of V. P. Singh as a possible alternative to Rajiv as national leader gave Zail Singh an opportunity to make a bid for a second term as President. His first term was to run out in July of 1987, and until the spring of that year there had been no chance that Rajiv and the Party would support him for a second. But then Zail Singh started badgering Rajiv. Late in April, he wrote to him demanding detailed technical information about the purchases of the West German submarines and the Bofors field guns. Rajiv lamely replied that he had laid before Parliament all the information he had. At the same time, Rajiv's advisers tried to put it about that Zail Singh couldn't be trusted as President, because he had been chief minister of Punjab and then Home Affairs Minister in the central government during the time when the Sikh secessionist movement took root. Some of them actually tried to link him with Indira Gandhi's assassination. He sought legal opinion on the extent of the President's constitutional powers, and started telling people openly that he had the right to dismiss a Prime Minister who was found to be corrupt, even if the Prime Minister enjoyed the confidence of Parliament. He met with lawyers, leaders of opposition parties, Congress dissidents in Parliament, and important journalists to see what support he could muster for dismissing Rajiv and having him prosecuted on charges of corruption—apparently, in return for their help in his own candidacy for a second term. It was rumored that a man who was a retired chief justice of the Supreme Court and a former law minister had actually written a speech for him to deliver after ousting Rajiv. Zail Singh's plan, it was said, was to call on V. P. Singh to form a new Cabinet, and give him six weeks or two months to do so and to get a vote of confidence in Parliament— enough time, presumably, for members of Parliament to forsake Rajiv for the new Prime Minister.

Early in May, however, the opposition parties announced that under the constitution the President could not dismiss the Prime Minister—an announcement that stayed Zail Singh's hand and averted a constitutional crisis. The opposition parties had various motives for their action, one of which appeared to be that they did not want to be beholden to Zail Singh. And they may have fancied that Rajiv could be dethroned by the mounting scandals without any push from the President. Anyway, they were all aware that if the President could dismiss a Congress Indira Prime Minister today he could dismiss a Janata Prime Minister, for instance, tomorrow; and they also had to be aware that if the President, the head of state, could overthrow the Prime Minister, the head of government, then one day an Army general could overthrow the head of state, and seize power. Such coups had been the fate of most poor countries, including Bangladesh and Pakistan, on India's very borders. Even so, the political atmosphere was so dangerous for Rajiv that he was said to have passed up his first choice for the Congress Indira Party's new candidate for President—B. Shankaranand, his Minister of Irrigation and Power, from Karnataka, who was known as "Rajiv's rubber stamp"—in favor of the current Vice-President, Ramaswamy Venkataraman, from Tamil Nadu, who was more independent-minded and acceptable. In June, Venkataraman was duly chosen by the Party as its candidate.

Zail Singh now started testing the waters to see whether the opposition parties and Congress dissidents would adopt him as their candidate. V. P. Singh, who might have led a rebellion against Rajiv, wouldn't play Zail Singh's game. He was known for being an upstanding man, and he shrank from the unseemly public spectacle of a President conspiring against a Prime Minister. Anyway, it seemed that he didn't want to take part in a back-stabbing scheme, and one that, furthermore, was promoted by a Congress apostate. V. P. Singh was also riding so high politically that he had reason to expect to come into the office of the Prime Minister in his own right in due course. Then, in late June, Zail Singh's ambitions were snuffed out, for the opposition parties adopted as their candidate V. Krishna Iyer, a retired justice of the Supreme Court from Tamil Nadu, to run against Venkataraman, and Iyer let it be known that he did not think the President had the right to dismiss the Prime Minister.

Zail Singh's failure did not bring any reprieve for Rajiv. The state elections in Haryana were scheduled for June 20th and 22nd, and Rajiv had already led Congress Indira to defeat in no fewer than nine states, one after another. Even without those losses, Haryana would have had a special importance for him, because the state, which was ruled by the Congress Indira Party, adjoined Delhi, and so was in his back yard, and it was an important state in the Hindi-speaking heartland, the traditional constituency of Congress. For some time now, Rajiv had seemed to side with Haryana against Punjab, and, as a result, any remaining moderate Sikhs who supported him felt betrayed. Indeed, he had ended up giving further impetus to the Sikh secessionist movement. He certainly campaigned vigorously in Haryana. One opposition candidate, Devi Lal, who was the leader of a party named Lok Dal, campaigned mainly on the issue of corruption in the central government; one of the Lok Dal slogans was "We don't want foreign wives, foreign money, or foreign banks." ("Foreign wives" was, of course, a pointed reference to Sonia's origins.) The Lok Dal put it about that the Bofors guns bought by Rajiv's government were defective. The rumor was especially harmful because many of the Haryana voters were Jats, and many Jats were in the military. When the election was held, Congress Indira was barely able to salvage half a dozen seats out of eighty, in what commentators called a "political hurricane." The state's Congress Indira chief minister, Bansi Lal, and all but one of his Congress ministers were unable to hold on to their seats. One devastating effect of the rout was that, with the loss of a Congress government in Haryana, Rajiv lost whatever leverage he had had in forcing a settlement on Haryana and Punjab, and thus Punjab threatened to become either a permanent battleground of religious warfare, as Northern Ireland is in the United Kingdom, or a separate country. In New Delhi, Congress Party dissidents in Parliament grew increasingly numerous and increasingly restive. They were kept from going over to the opposition only by a recent anti-defection law, which required a member to stand for reëlection whenever he or she switched parties. The Presidential election was held three weeks after the defeat in Haryana. Venkataraman was easily elected, but Rajiv immediately expelled three Congress dissidents—Arun Nehru, V. C. Shukla, and Arif Muhammad Khan—from the Party, for trying to recruit others to their ranks during the campaign. Arun Singh, a fourth dissident, at once resigned his post in protest. Arun Nehru, the Minister of Internal Security, and Arun Singh, the Minister of State for Defense, were perhaps two of the closest friends and advisers Rajiv had ever had, and they, along with V. C. Shukla and Arif Muhammad Khan (until he resigned over the Muslim Women's bill), had been among the most prominent members of Rajiv's government, and, previously, of his mother's. The following day, V. P. Singh sent this telegram to Rajiv: "The message is loud and clear, that any Congressman can be politically hanged without a hearing, or any specific reason. . . . If throwing me out of the party will help the party, I am ready to offer this supreme political sacrifice by submitting my resignation."

Ever since the German-submarine scandal, Rajiv had been under pressure from Congress Indira officials to expel V. P. Singh from the Party. Rajiv had desisted not only because V. P. Singh was perhaps the most popular member of his besieged government but also because he didn't want to deepen suspicions of an ever-thickening coverup. In any case, after receiving V. P. Singh's telegram Rajiv dillydallied for several days and then accepted his resignation. At the same time, as if trying to counter the impression that he had no intention of putting his house in order, he forced the film actor Amitabh Bachchan to resign from his seat in the Parliament.

Even before the eruption of the scandals, Rajiv had frittered away the capital of his victory by backing off from bold political initiatives as soon as they met with a little resistance, by treating his Party colleagues with disrespect, by ignoring governmental institutions and institutional procedures, and, as people liked to say, by "shuffling his Cabinet like a pack of cards." (In his four years, he had changed the composition of his Cabinet no fewer than twenty-four times.) He had acquired a reputation for being secretive, for not answering letters, for avoiding journalists—for keeping very much to himself and his family. Unlike previous Prime Ministers, he had no confidants in either the political or the civil establishment. Instead, he relied on just three or four school chums, who, as the *Times of India* noted, amused him and ran errands for him and, in the process, became rich. He had lost his credibility and, with it, his ability to govern, because unless the masses

respected—indeed, stood in awe of—what was called the "stick"
no one could wield it effectively and control the large, turbulent
country.

Around the end of February, 1988, Zail Singh, now a private
citizen, casually let drop to a New Delhi journalist the fact that
some people, whom he didn't name, had offered him three or four
hundred million rupees (or thirty or forty million dollars) to wage
his campaign for a second term—an offer that, he said, he had
refused. The remark set off a new political storm. Congress dissidents and opposition politicians started accusing each other of
trying to bribe the President—a charge that was rather like the pot
calling the kettle black. In any case, the possibility that the whole
political process, and not just Rajiv's government, might be corrupt was suddenly brought into the open, and Rajiv was quick to
seize the opportunity to praise Zail Singh for making the offer
public and calling it to the government's notice. It was as though
he could finally portray himself in the role of judge rather than that
of defendant. The editors of *The Illustrated Weekly of India* inter-
viewed Zail Singh about the bribe, and when they asked who had
offered it to him he said, "Wait for the right moment. I don't want
any more trouble now. . . . I'll reveal the truth one day and you'll
be all surprised."

When V. P. Singh was forced out of the Cabinet, in April,
1987, he was very careful not to distance himself in any way from
the Congress Party. In fact, he was at pains to present himself as
someone who had been ousted because he chose to be loyal to time-
honored Congress principles and policies instead of to an individual. When, a few months later, he was forced to leave the Party, he
was seen as a victim of Rajiv's self-serving action more than as
someone who had betrayed Party principles. He was generally
regarded as a casualty of his own campaign to sweep away the muck

of scandals, and thus as the rightful heir to Rajiv's titles as both Mr. Clean and Prime Minister.

In June, 1988, V. P. Singh stood as a united-opposition candidate in a by-election for Amitabh Bachchan's seat, in Allahabad. Although the significance of the election was somewhat diminished by the fact that at the last minute Bachchan failed to stand against Singh, and so deprived him of the benefit of a head-to-head contest on the issue of corruption, that issue was the focus of the campaign and was the source of the big victory Singh subsequently obtained: he defeated his nearest rival—Sunil Shastri (the son of the former Prime Minister Lal Bahadur Shastri), who was running as the Congress Party candidate—by more than two to one. (During the victory celebration, Singh's supporters shouted, "Bring back the nation's money to the country! Rajiv Gandhi, return to your senses!") Singh's victory was one of a series of opposition victories in by-elections, and these were seen, at least by the opposition parties, as an omen of what awaited Rajiv in the general election, which he was required under the constitution to call before December, 1989, when the sitting Parliament's mandate would run out.

But V. P. Singh, in contrast to Rajiv, was an unknown quantity when it came to getting votes in a national election. His platform consisted of little more than nationalist, populist, and anti-business speeches. His strongest suit was his modest, self-effacing character (after his victory in Allahabad he said that it would be a "disaster" for the country if he became Prime Minister), but in the cutthroat world of Indian politics that could be as much a disadvantage as an advantage. Moreover, the opposition parties, his only probable supporters, were, as always, somewhat divided, and anyway opposition parties had been able to win a majority in Parliament against the Congress Party only once—in 1977, when, uniting to run against Mrs. Gandhi's generally hated Emergency, they elected a Janata government. But they weren't able to stay united, and remained in power only eighteen months. Even if Singh could somehow unite the opposition parties behind him, he would face the problem of getting more experienced opposition politicians, like Chandra Shekhar and Ramakrishna Hegde, to subordinate their ambitions to his.

The issue of corruption, which had been the preoccupation of politics in India for nearly two years, continued to reverberate as the dominant theme of Rajiv's Prime Ministership. On September 6th, journalists all across the country went on a one-day strike to protest a government measure intended to silence future reports of corruption or of the misuse of power by government officials which had just been rushed through the lower house of Parliament. But the issue of corruption, though serious, was a distraction from the country's grave long-term problems: the need for birth control; terrorism in Punjab and Assam; the revolt against any kind of meaningful land reform by local landowners in various parts of the country; Hindu-Muslim riots; the violence of martial Gurkhas in West Bengal; the involvement of Indian troops in the ethnic conflict in Sri Lanka; the possible nuclear threat from Pakistan; and, overriding everything else, the neglect of the basic needs of the people. It was also a distraction from such immediate concerns as the sudden death of President Zia-ul-Haq of Pakistan, in August; the recent earthquake in Bihar; and the floods in September in Bangladesh, which inundated a third of the country and threatened to start a new influx of refugees into India. And it was a distraction from Rajiv's one indisputable achievement, which might have assured him a place in history: the loosening of governmental economic controls, which released a potent, almost explosive energy, and perhaps set the stage for a new era of private industry and a new generation of entrepreneurs. Meanwhile, many thoughtful people firmly maintained that the Congress Indira Party was no more corrupt than any party in power would be, and that, whatever the political and moral stature of V. P. Singh, the Party and the family that had ruled the country for most of its independent life remained the best hope for the survival of Indian democracy.

8

The Assassination
and the General Election

The second general election in the Prime Ministership of Rajiv
Gandhi was held in November, 1989, and was fought between
Rajiv and V. P. Singh, essentially on the issue of the Bofors scandal.
(The scandal remains mired in investigation, not just in India but
also in Switzerland, where the Federal Court dismissed only in July,
1993, a challenge intended to prevent access to secret Swiss accounts. As a self-serving spokesman of Bofors put it, what had
happened "belongs already to history.") This time, Congress Indira
was as badly defeated as it had been gloriously successful in the
previous election; it won only a hundred and ninety-seven seats in
the lower house of Parliament out of five hundred and forty-five.
Although the Janata Dal Socialists, V. P. Singh's party, secured even
fewer seats—only a hundred and forty-two—he was able to form a
minority government, thanks to the opportunistic support of other
small parties. (One minor oddity of the election was that Maneka
Gandhi was elected from the constituency of Pilibhit, in Uttar
Pradesh, and became not only a member of Parliament but also a
junior minister of Environment and Forests—a post she was given
primarily, it seemed, to annoy the rest of the Gandhi family.)

As Prime Minister, V. P. Singh sought to better the lot of the
poor by extending to what were designated Other Backward Classes
the constitutional affirmative-action program that reserved twenty-

Rajiv Gandhi. Campaign trail, 1990. (S. K. Chadha.)

two and a half per cent of the jobs in central and state governments for Untouchables, irrespective of individual merit. His change would have meant that an additional twenty-seven per cent of those government jobs would be reserved for minorities. (According to the last available census, Untouchables number a hundred and fifty-four million; no such count exists for Other Backward Classes, for the simple reason that the classification is mostly an invention of poor peoples trying to lay claim to the reservations.) The mere threat of an affirmative-action program on such a large scale provoked a bitter protest by the majority, consisting of people who were, of couse, relatively well off. The ensuing strife and disorder resulted in the downfall of Singh's government after just eleven months in office. That government was succeeded in November, 1990, by another minority government, led by Chandra Shekhar, the former president of the Janata Party, who had made a career of defecting from various parties. Chandra Shekhar at once abandoned any idea of expanding the program. Eventually, however, the protest movement spent itself and the well-off people became resigned, whereupon, in 1993, the legislation expanding the program to forty-nine and a half per cent was finally enacted into law.

Chandra Shekhar's government was made up largely of defectors from Singh's Janata Dal Socialists, and Singh himself, of course, had been a defector from the Congress Party, so the new leader's hold on power was no more secure than Singh's. Chandra Shekhar functioned merely as a caretaker Prime Minister until the following May, when another general election was held.

This was India's tenth general election, and Monday, May 20th, was the day of polling in New Delhi. Two additional election days, the twenty-third and the twenty-sixth, were scheduled in other parts of the country, polling being a cumbersome process in India. The election bore close watching, for in the past months the country had been going through much political, economic, and religious turmoil. On the Monday of the New Delhi voting, I was visiting the city, and I accompanied a friend to her polling place, a college building.

Outside, in the hot sun, half a dozen political workers were lounging at two tables set up near the entrance. Behind one table, two posters bearing the red-white-and-green symbol of the "Congress (I) Party" were mounted high on the façade. One poster attacked the caretaker government of Chandra Shekhar by showing a shattered clay piggy bank spilling out coins, with a caption asking "What sort of government came, broke the banks, and brought a price rise?" followed by the exhortation "Bring back Congress (I)." The other poster had a picture of Rajesh Khanna, the local Congress Indira candidate for Parliament, along with the Party slogan, "For Stability and Progress." Hanging from a bamboo pole beneath the posters was the Congress (I) flag, bearing the Party symbol of a hand held up in greeting.

High on the façade behind the other table was an orange-red poster for the conservative, Hindu-revivalist Bharatiya Janata

Party, showing a lotus, an ancient Hindu symbol; beside the stem was the name of the Party's candidate for Parliament, L. K. Advani, and at the top was the injunction "Vote B.J.P." A flag hung beneath this poster, too—the Bharatiya Janata Party's orange-and-green one, also bearing a lotus. The table held brochures giving the highlights of the Party program, in English, under titles like "Towards Rama Rajya" (the "rule of Rama," which Hindus regard as the Golden Age), "Clean Political System," "Economic Growth with Social Justice," "Vibrant Social Order," and "World Fraternity." The Bharatiya Janata Party was emerging as the main opposition of the Congress Party, which, in its different guises, had now ruled the country for forty of the forty-four years since Independence.

I asked my friend why political parties were allowed to campaign at the polling station, and she said, "They are supposedly here to make sure that there is no hanky-panky. But, of course, in a lot of places they themselves are responsible for all kinds of booth-capturing." The term "booth-capturing" covered a multitude of electoral violations, from terrorizing would-be voters to stuffing ballot boxes.

Inside the polling station were more tables, these manned by election officials and clerks, but hardly anyone was waiting to vote. My friend presented a voter-registration slip to the official who had the register of voters, and he handed her a ballot. With a toothpick that had been dipped in indelible ink, the official put a mark on the nail of my friend's right forefinger—a routine procedure to prevent people from voting twice.

My friend and I walked to the back of the room, where the ballot box—a steel box the size of a small trunk, with a foot-long slot at the top, and a government seal—stood on a table. Around the table was a makeshift cardboard partition that barely screened my friend from the people in the room. "At the last election, they had a proper screen," she told me. Then she unfolded the ballot paper. It was nearly a yard long and two feet wide, and on it, in each of four panels, were listed seventeen or eighteen of a total of seventy candidates for the New Delhi Parliamentary constituency. (In other parts of the country, elections for state assemblies were also being held, but New Delhi is not a part of a state; it is a union territory and is directly governed by the central government.) Each panel of the ballot paper was subdivided into five columns, with headings for each candidate's name, address, party affiliation, symbol, and symbol number. The information was printed in Hindi, Urdu, and English—the languages spoken in New Delhi—and the symbols were there because more than half of the Indian electorate was illiterate and depended on them to identify the candidates. Many of the party symbols were familiar from posters and flags around the city: a dress for the Samdarshi Party, an elephant for the Bahujan Samaj Party, a hoe for the Poorvanchal Rashtriya Congress, a boy pouring water for the Doordarshi, a radio for the Bhartiya Loktantrik Mazdoor Dal, a man driving oxen for the Lok Dal, a bicycle for the J & K Panthers Party, a wheel for the Janata Dal, an apple for the Desh Bhakt Party, a torch for the Jan Parishad, and, of course, the hand for the Congress Party and the lotus for the Bharatiya Janata Party.

In the country at large, thirty-eight parties were fielding candidates for five hundred and eleven seats in the lower house of Parliament. (In some states, violence on the part of religious extremists had made it necessary to postpone the elections.) In addition to sixteen candidates endorsed by the parties on my friend's ballot, there were fifty-four independent candidates, each listed with his own symbol. Their symbols, too, were taken mostly from everyday life, and included a trumpet, a conch shell, an airplane, an anchor, a jeep, a telephone, an easel, a drum, a light bulb, a table fan, a ceiling fan, a fire engine, a handcart, a train, and a teacup.

I asked whether the ballot couldn't have been made simpler.

"You'll be surprised to learn that in some parts of the South the ballot paper is twice as big as this one—with twice as many candidates," my friend said.

"How can voters find their way around in such chaos?" I asked. "It's hard to see how illiterate voters could manage to pick out the symbols for the candidates of their choice."

"No one cares," she said. "In this blessed country, anyone can stand as an independent candidate merely by paying a security deposit of five hundred rupees and getting a symbol approved by the Election Commission." The Election Commission, a body that is appointed by the government but is independent of it, is charged with supervising the election. Five hundred rupees was about twenty dollars in 1991. "Apparently, in this election there are almost nine thousand candidates standing for the Lok Sabha and almost seventeen thousand for the state assemblies. The only way to reduce the number of candidates would be to raise the security deposit."

"Why hasn't that been done?"

"Recently, there was a proposal to raise it to fifty thousand rupees, but the politicians derailed it—God knows why. All over the country, people are taking longer and longer to cast their votes."

"But here there is hardly anybody waiting to vote," I said.

"Half the people are so disgusted with all the governments that they are staying away," my friend said.

She picked up from the table a little wooden stamp with a rubber cross on it, inked it on a pad, and put the mark on the lotus. Then, though she carefully refolded the ballot paper along the creases, she still had to struggle to push it through the slot in the ballot box.

May and June are generally the hottest months in New Delhi: the city bakes in kiln-like heat until relief comes with the monsoon rains of July and August. In 1991, however, in the early evening on the twenty-first of May—the day after its election day—the city was battered for more than an hour by strong winds and hailstones the size of golf balls. Roads became waterlogged, trees were uprooted, and overhead power cables snapped. A boy was electrocuted by a fallen cable. A man was struck dead by a bolt of lightning. At least a dozen people were injured. My bearer in the hotel told me he had said an extra prayer, because he was sure that the unseasonable storm was a bad omen.

Around eleven o'clock, the bearer woke me up to give me the news that Rajiv Gandhi had been killed in a bomb blast. "I hope it's not a Sikh, or the city will be drowned in the blood of the Sikhs," he said.

I was stunned by the news. I told the bearer that I shared his apprehension, and said I wondered if the assassinations and violence would make Indians lose faith in democracy.

"Why, Sahib?" he said. "The Mogul courts were full of intrigues and murders. Royal brothers cut each other's throats, sons killed their fathers—that's the way our governments have always worked."

When he left to give the news to other guests, I turned on the radio, and caught the eleven-thirty news broadcast from All-India Radio, which gave the circumstances of Rajiv's assassination. He had been killed during a campaign stop in Sriperumbudur, near Madras, in South India. A woman with explosives strapped to her waist had approached him as if to touch his feet in a gesture of obeisance and had set off the explosives. She and thirteen bystanders had also died. The station went off the air for the night immediately after the news broadcast, as usual—without so much as a recapitulation of Rajiv's life. I switched on the television, but it, too, was just going off the air. (At the time, there was only one national television channel in India, and both it and All-India Radio were run by the government.) The shutdown of both radio and television at such a moment was eerie; after all, Rajiv was at the time of his death the president of the Congress Indira Party and had served the country from 1984 to 1989 as its Prime Minister. In the subsequent days, it became clear that the broadcast authorities had been afraid that in the middle of the elections any discussion of Rajiv's life and death might be construed as political propaganda for the Congress Indira Party. In the Western press, however, perhaps partly because Rajiv was the young, handsome scion of the best-known Indian family in the world, and perhaps also because he was interested in Western technology and ideas, his assassination was given a great deal of coverage. By comparison, reactions in India seemed restrained.

After the assault on the Golden Temple, Rajiv had been the special quarry of the Sikh extremists: they blamed him for not bringing to book the Congress Indira culprits who had incited the anti-Sikh rioters following Mrs. Gandhi's death—and, in fact, no action was ever taken against them. In consequence, the cordon of security around him—not only while he was Prime Minister but also after the election of 1989—had been unprecedented. Yet by the time of the election campaign of 1991 the security had been relaxed, either because he and his advisers thought he shouldn't appear remote from the electorate or because they thought that with the passing of time the Sikh threat had diminished, and during the weeks leading up to the election he had been mingling freely with the crowds.

The day after the assassination, the city was abuzz with rumors about who was responsible for it. Sikh terrorists and other extremist groups were mentioned, of course, but one rumor focussed on the opposition Bharatiya Janata Party, which had helped first V. P. Singh and then Chandra Shekhar to become Prime Minister. "He was the only person who stood between the Party and its dream of creating a Hindu society" is how the argument went. Another rumor had it that "the foreign hand" was involved. "The C.I.A. has struck again to destabilize our country and keep us weak," the nationalists contended, as usual.

Among the journalists I met on my rounds, there was a considerable flap about reports that a number of friends of India and of the Gandhi family, including Kenneth D. Kaunda, Julius K. Nyerere, Daniel Ortega, Willy Brandt, and Brian Mulroney, were not coming to New Delhi for the cremation. It had been learned that various high officials in Britain were not coming, either (since, after all, Rajiv was not the head of the government), so there was great relief at the news that Prince Charles would come, in a special

R.A.F. plane; Rajiv had attended the Prince's wedding, and they had had personal ties. And then it turned out that Douglas Hurd, Britain's Foreign Secretary, would come, too; he was hitching a ride with Prince Charles.

Within a couple of days, it became clear that Rajiv's assassination had been carried out by members of the Liberation Tigers of Tamil Eelam, popularly known as the Tamil Tigers—a secessionist Tamil group in Sri Lanka. The group had been fighting a guerrilla war in northern and eastern Sri Lanka for more than twenty-five years. In Sri Lanka, Tamils, who were Hindus and were in the minority, had long felt that the Sinhalese, who were Buddhists and were in the majority, treated them as second-class citizens, and they resented their treatment even more keenly after the fifties, when Sinhalese was made the official language. The history of the Indian government's relations with the Tamil Tigers in Mrs. Gandhi's time was complicated, and was not unlike the history of its relations with the Sikh extremists. Although she outwardly maintained good relations with Sri Lanka, she followed a policy of secretly arming the Tamil Tigers in their struggle. Her motives were a matter of speculation. Perhaps she was trying to keep Sri Lanka unstable, and thus dependent on India. Perhaps she wanted to help protect the three million Tamils of Sri Lanka in order to win favor with fifty million Tamils living in South India, mostly in the state of Tamil Nadu. (The village where Rajiv Gandhi was killed is in Tamil Nadu.) Or perhaps she was disturbed by the flow of Tamils migrating from Sri Lanka. It was estimated that there were a hundred and fifteen thousand Tamil refugees from Sri Lanka living in camps in Tamil Nadu, and that perhaps as many more were living elsewhere in the state, illegally, and were engaged in small businesses, like hawking wares on the street. All these refugees served as a constant reminder to Indian Tamils of their brothers' and sisters' struggles on the neighboring island. Whatever Mrs. Gandhi's motives were, her policy backfired. By the time Rajiv took office, the Tamils in Sri Lanka were so strong that they threatened to dismember the country. Rajiv feared that other powers would therefore come to the aid of the Sri Lankan government, and so upstage India. There was also the danger that if the Tamil rebellion succeeded in Sri Lanka it might incite rebellion among Tamils within India, and such a rebellion might split north from south and culminate in the breakup of the union.

In 1987, Rajiv made an agreement with the government of Sri Lanka to provide Indian troops to crush the Tamil rebellion within its borders, and at one point in the following year there were as many as seventy thousand Indian troops in Sri Lanka. Rajiv thereby earned the enmity not only of the Tamils but also of the Sinhalese, for they came to regard the Indian troops as an occupying force. In fact, while Rajiv was in Colombo to sign the agreement a Sinhalese soldier in the Guard of Honor was seized in the act of hitting him with the butt of his rifle. Many Indians feared that Sri Lanka could become India's Vietnam: Indian troops were having little success against the Tamil guerrillas, and the Sri Lankan government was losing popularity at home and was coming under attack by a Sinhalese Maoist group. In 1988, the Sri Lankan government asked Rajiv to withdraw his troops, and he had little choice but to acquiesce. His policy toward the Tamils, like his mother's, had backfired. Both Indira Gandhi and Rajiv had made the mistake of confusing short-term political considerations with the long-term interests of the country. The Tamil Tigers blamed Rajiv for undermining their near-revolution in Sri Lanka, and they also claimed that as a consequence of his intervention their cause had suffered an international eclipse.

On the twenty-second of May, the Congress Indira Working Committee, meeting in New Delhi under the chairmanship of P. V. Narasimha Rao, unanimously elected Sonia Gandhi, the widow of Rajiv, to succeed her husband as the Party president, and as it did so Congress workers gathered outside her residence and chanted slogans like "Save the country! Bring in Sonia Gandhi!" When the Party spokesman, Pranab Mukherjee, was asked if Sonia had been consulted, he said, "There is no question of her refusing. She is a Party member, and the decision will be communicated to her in due course." The reason that political observers gave for her selection was that the Congress Indira Party wanted to make the most of "the sympathy factor." Its touchstone was, of course, the sympathy vote for her husband, some six years earlier. The choice was nevertheless remarkable, on several counts: though Sonia Gandhi had become a naturalized Indian in 1983, some fifteen years after her marriage to Rajiv, she was born and brought up in Italy, and she was a Roman Catholic; she had never evinced any interest in politics; and there was no tradition in India of drafting a reluctant politician for office, not to mention a grieving widow. Many of the people on the Working Committee who supported her selection were close family friends, and should presumably have known better than to put her in such an awkward position.

Sonia firmly turned down the offer, not once but twice, and eventually P. V. Narasimha Rao himself was elected the Party's president. He was a seasoned and respected leader, but he was seventy years old and had had multiple-bypass heart surgery. The Gandhi coterie began projecting Rajiv's daughter, Priyanka, who was nineteen years old, as a future leader of the Congress Indira Party. Rajiv's son, Rahul, who was twenty, was a student at Harvard and, it was said, had never shown any interest in politics.

On May 24th, the cortege and the cremation took place in New Delhi, on the banks of the Yamuna River. People would long remember Rajiv's funeral—for the heat, the crowds, and, above all, the heavy stillness in the air. There is something elemental about the Hindu last rites, in contrast with those in the West, where death is handled so discreetly. On that oppressive day in May, the cremation's primitiveness and finality were riveting: the exposed body on the funeral pyre; the wood being arranged and rearranged on top of the body; the son and heir, Rahul, lighting the pyre with a taper; and then the burst of flames.

"So vast is the Indian electoral exercise, arguably the biggest voluntary mobilisation in the world of men, women and materials for a single objective, that there is a sense of marvel that it culminates with so little disruption of life and with limited violence," a New Delhi newspaper called the *Business & Political Observer* noted a few days after the general election of 1991 began. Of course, everyone agrees that the Indian general election is an enormous achievement. Among other things, hundreds of millions of ballot papers must be individually unfolded, examined, and counted by hand. (For security reasons, the officials who count the ballots sit in locked cages, under the eyes of suspicious functionaries of various parties.) But elections in India have always been marred by intimidation and violence of many varieties. Even before the assassination, the general election of 1991 was threatening to be the most violent one ever. In New Delhi, Sikh terrorist gangs riding in stolen cars tried to assassinate Sajjan Kumar and Jagdish Tytler, two Congress Indira Party candidates for Parliament from New Delhi, who were well-known friends of the Gandhi family; the Sikhs believed that Tytler was one of the people who had masterminded the riots following Mrs. Gandhi's death. Both men escaped unharmed, but several members of their bodyguards were killed. (Although New Delhi has an elaborate system of red alerts and other security drills, and although there are so many police to be seen there that one has the feeling of being in an armed camp, the would-be assassins managed to escape without anyone's giving chase, firing at them, or stopping them at any of the capital's innumerable roadblocks.) In Meerut, in Uttar Pradesh, nineteen people were killed in Hindu-Muslim riots. To restore calm, the authorities imposed a dusk-to-dawn curfew there, and they were also doing so in many other riot-torn towns. In Jehanabad, in Bihar, just after the polling began, a gang of armed men who were said to be Congress Indira Party supporters surrounded the polling station, threw stones at the assembled voters, and fired shots into the air. The gang then stormed the polling station, snatched the ballot papers from the presiding election officer, and stamped the symbol of the hand on them. Nearly a hundred booths in and around Jehanabad were similarly captured. In another town in Bihar, three hundred incidents of booth-capturing were reported, and there were stories of such incidents of electoral violence scattered across the country. The Election Commission was monitoring the violence and ordering repolling in these constituencies as best it could.

Because of the assassination, the two election days remaining were postponed until June 12th and June 15th except in Punjab; there the election was put off until September. The Punjab election campaign had already claimed the lives of twenty-three candidates and hundreds of voters; in fact, Congress candidates did not stand in the state, for fear of being murdered. In the country as a whole, the tally of people killed as a result of polling had risen above eight hundred by the fifteenth of June. The figure exceeded by far that for any previous election, yet this election had the lowest turnout of any since 1957—only fifty-three per cent of the eligible voters.

Even so, the 1991 electoral exercise was not without its positive aspects. Elections in India are generally considered an accurate gauge of the people's will, and this election, despite all the chaos at the polls, was no exception. In almost every state, two dominant parties emerged for the first time—but different pairs of parties in different states. Also, in the past one of the weaknesses of Indian politics had been widespread defections—people changing party affiliations, horse-trading, breaking away from parties to form new ones—in order to win positions of power. In the 1991 election, many such defectors went down to defeat. Among them were Devi Lal, the Deputy Prime Minister; Maneka Gandhi; and a host of other government ministers.

Some of the election results were predictable, such as the victory in West Bengal of the Communist Party of India (Marxist), which, after initially splitting off as a pro-Chinese faction from the pro-Soviet Communist Party of India, in 1964, had gone on to win four successive general elections in the state over two decades—increasingly portraying itself as an independent party with links to neither the Chinese nor the Soviet Communists. Equally predictable was the victory of V. P. Singh and the Janata Dal Socialists in Bihar, which, possibly next to Orissa, is the poorest state. But other results were unsettling. For instance, the Congress Indira was put to rout in the north. Yet it did so well in the south (partly as a consequence of the sympathy factor) that it chalked up a total of two hundred and twenty-two seats in the lower house of Parliament, which left it and its post-electoral allies—a number of small parties gravitated to it, because no party wanted still another general election—only about thirty seats short of a majority. The Congress Indira was therefore able to form a minority government, with P. V. Narasimha Rao as the Prime Minister. (Arjun Singh, the boss of Madhya Pradesh, replaced him as the president of the Party.) Rao was a veteran of the governments of Mrs. Gandhi and Rajiv—he had served in the Cabinets of both, holding important portfolios, such as that of External Affairs—and his selection was seen as an attempt by the Gandhi coterie to keep the old Congress order in place. Sharad Pawar, a bitter rival of Rao's in the Congress Indira Party, was named to the important position of Minister of Defense, as part of his price for allowing Rao to become Prime Minister. All the same, the Congress government looked weak; the Bharatiya Janata Party, now its main opposition, seemed to be waiting in the wings to become the ruling party.

The Bharatiya Janata Party had won only two seats in the lower house of Parliament in 1984, but in 1989 it had won eighty-eight. That was a big jump, and in 1991 it won a hundred and nineteen seats. Indeed, many observers maintained that the Bharatiya Janata Party might well have beaten the Congress Indira if it hadn't been for Rajiv's death in the middle of the election: in the first round, in which votes were cast for forty per cent of the seats, Congress Indira did much worse than in the second and third rounds, and only then pulled ahead. Moreover, the Bharatiya Janata Party captured four important states in the north, including Uttar Pradesh, the base of the Nehru-Gandhi family and the largest state in India's heartland. Despite that strong showing, however, the Bharatiya Janata Party's appeal was essentially regional. All its members ever elected to Parliament came from the north and northwest of India—ninety per cent of them from eight of the country's thirty-two states and union territories, and forty per cent from Uttar Pradesh alone.

The Bharatiya Janata Party, which grew out of right-wing Hindu-chauvinist movements that came into being at the time of the Partition and Independence, was so stridently pro-Hindu when it was established, in the early eighties, that it didn't even pay lip service to the principle of secularism. During the 1991 election, some of its leaders did moderate their speeches enough so that they sounded like nationalists rather than like Hindu chauvinists, but others kept up what sounded like a Fascist clamor: in campaign speeches Bal Thackeray, a leader of Shiv Sena, which is a paramilitary Hindu-extremist group allied with the Bharatiya Janata Party, chilled many Hindus and Muslims by blaming Mahatma Gandhi for the Partition of India and honoring his assassin, Nathuram Godse.

Indians are very sensitive to what is said about them in the Western press, and especially in the British press; and at the time of Rajiv's death people in government and university circles were quite exercised over articles and editorials in British publications suggesting that the British influence in India had only recently ended and the consequence was that the country was reverting to a divisive, even an anarchic, period. Those articles, which amounted to obituaries of "Raj India," argued that the Raj had not ended with Independence, in 1947, but continued right up to the defeat of Rajiv Gandhi's government, in 1989, with Indian leaders and officials having merely taken over the Empire's trappings of power. They said that the underpinnings of the Indian government after

Independence had remained, for the most part, those of the British Raj: a professional civil service, an independent judiciary, and a professional Army, all animated, one way or another, by British ideals. The almost successive electoral victories of the Congress Party led by Nehru, his daughter, and her son, under the banners of secularism and socialism, were interpreted as little more than plebiscites on their rule.

"The Nehru Dynasty" ruled the country for a total of thirty-eight years, enjoying powers akin to those of the viceroys, the articles said, and under the Dynasty the administrative apparatus of the British Raj was not only maintained but made to serve the family's economic policy. They went on to say that Nehru misguidedly attempted to graft a Soviet-style system of economic planning onto the existing Indian economy, and that the attempt resulted in a crushing political, administrative, and economic centralization of a country with a great diversity of peoples; and that Mrs. Gandhi, carrying her father's centralization even further, dealt the coup de grâce to the independence of both the civil service and the judiciary by thoroughly politicizing them. An editorial in the London *Financial Times* declared that "the Raj is now nearing collapse," and argued that India's overcentralized government had created its own antithesis, in the form of "regional separatism, Hindu revivalism, political fragmentation and economic disarray." The editorial also noted that Rajiv, V. P. Singh, and Chandra Shekhar had all tried, in their different ways, to change things around, but in vain—for all three remained the children of the Congress Party, and tinkered with the system but didn't seriously try to reform it—and that the Bharatiya Janata Party could not come up with a solution, either. The *Financial Times* then offered its own remedy: "To remain democratic, a country as vast as India must become a loose federation. . . . Economic liberalism is itself a form of decentralisation. But it is also one that would allow the combination of economic integration with local political autonomy."

Of all the articles that appeared around the time of the election, the one that was perhaps the most widely read and discussed was a comprehensive and searching treatment of India's economic problems which appeared in *The Economist* in May. It argued that the Indian economy since Independence had been shackled by an extraordinary combination of extreme protectionism and domestic regulation, the reason being that the Indian government had pursued a policy of economic self-sufficiency, and so had chosen to have many capital goods, like heavy machinery, and nearly all consumer goods produced within the country, even if those goods were of lower quality than their competitors in the world market. The economy had long been virtually closed to international trade, and India had charged extremely high tariffs on all foreign goods. Furthermore, before imports could even reach the tariff barrier they were faced with a complex and seemingly irrational system of classification and licensing. (A similar system applied to domestic products.) The main—unstated—purpose of the licensing system was to support a kind of distributive politics that allowed politicians at the center and in the states to provide for their supporters by insuring that there were always plenty of bribes to go around. As a consequence of the protectionism and the licensing, India imported almost no consumer goods. The effect of such a policy was to hamper growth and prevent the country from achieving its full economic potential: India's population was four times that of the Americas, yet its gross national product was about the same as that of Holland. "It is as absurd for India to pursue self-sufficiency as it would be for Spain or Switzerland," the article noted. "The world can get along fine without India, but India cannot prosper without the world." *The Economist* declared the results for the economy disastrous: "The inefficiencies caused by protection and badly run state enterprises are doubled and redoubled by the domestic regulatory system. This has no equal in the world. In many ways it puts Soviet central planning to shame."

Yet, it went on to say, India's success in controlling imports did not mean a corresponding increase in exports of manufactured goods. Between 1980 and 1985, the average annual growth rate for the volume of such exports was only one-tenth of one per cent. The slight liberalization of India's economy under Rajiv Gandhi, which began in 1985, had a startling effect on exports: the rate of growth between 1985 and 1988 jumped to 12.8 per cent. Nevertheless, India still lagged behind many other countries; South Korea, for example, had a growth rate of 23.9 per cent over the same period.

Continuing, the article said that, while the Indian government chose to act in the industrial sector, where its actions proved self-defeating, it ignored the real difference it could have made in the agricultural sector by alleviating rural poverty. The government's protectionist policy actually harmed rural areas, where most of the Indian poor live: by raising the domestic price of manufactured goods relative to that of agricultural goods, protectionism reduced the real income of the rural sector. And capital investment in agriculture declined; real investment in irrigation in India's largest states, for example, fell by eight per cent during the nineteen-eighties.

The Economist concluded that the only way for India to move forward economically was to abandon the cherished socialist policies and socialist nostrums of the Nehru Dynasty: "The government must dismantle an unbelievably complicated system of restraints and rewards that, over the past four decades, has securely enclosed every aspect of Indian life. The first and necessary step is to see these restraints and rewards as the cage that they are." The article noted that Indians living abroad were enterprising and successful in every area of life, and suggested that Indians at home would be equally successful if they were given half a chance. But the changes in India would have to be "not far short of a revolution" for that to happen. "The main prescription for policy is easy enough: India must be opened up to the rest of the world; the state must withdraw from micro-managing the economy and concentrate instead on building the social and physical infrastructure that the country lacks. . . . Left to arrange their own economic future, India's remarkable people would undoubtedly thrive. They have nothing to fear from competition or from the uncertainties of an unplanned world."

Influential people in India, by and large, said that many of the *The Economist's* points were well taken. There seemed to be general agreement with the journal's criticism of India's agricultural policy. At the same time, these people took exception to the basis of the analysis. Nehru's apologists said that the intent of his socialist policies was honorable—to prevent the exploitation of the poor by the rich, and to try to insure equitable distribution of such goods and services as were available in a poor country—and that anyway socialism, in one form or another, was the prevailing philosophy of many European governments in that period. (Since the collapse of the Soviet Union, opinion everywhere, of course, has shifted toward a market economy.)

A more important reservation made about the article was that it failed to take into account the fact that the underdeveloped countries it held up to India as examples, such as South Korea, Taiwan, and Malaysia, were much smaller than India and, moreover, all had highly authoritarian forms of government. It was also argued that if the Indian government had gone over to a market economy many of the poor would now be worse off than they were to start with. And many people said that, even if the long-term prescriptions of *The Economist* were right, they could not be adopted, because the whole democratic political apparatus was oiled by short-term considerations: the exchange of money at every stage of granting licenses filled the coffers of the parties and made campaigns and elections possible. Certainly it was hard to see how the parties and the elections could be financed without this system.

By the beginning of the nineties, India's civil service, its judiciary, and its other once stable, autonomous governing institutions had been compromised to the point where they were mere appurtenances of politicians. Corruption and intimidation at every level of society had brought into being a new moneyed class, which exercised ruthless power. Examples of corruption abounded. One story concerned Sharad Pawar and the wedding he held for his daughter, in Bombay, in 1991, when he was chief minister of Maharashtra. It was said that at least a million dollars was spent on the occasion—a large sum for a wedding anywhere, and, in a country with a per-capita income of three hundred and twenty-seven dollars a year, a staggering one. Of course, no money actually changed hands: people just got the idea of the kind of wedding his daughter should have, and everything was made available. (This outrageous event did not impede in any way his subsequent rise to high office in Rao's government.)

The well-known 1992 bank-securities racket, in which the flamboyant thirty-eight-year-old Bombay stockbroker Harshad Mehta, his family, and their business associates borrowed, with the apparent collusion of top bankers and bureaucrats, the improbable sum of one billion six hundred million dollars from banks to buy securities for him and unnamed clients of his, and pumped up the Bombay Stock Exchange to dizzying heights, quadrupling its share prices in a year, eclipsed all previous scandals. When the bubble burst, in April of that year, millions of investors lost their life savings. What means the associates used to persuade the banks to make them unbelievably large loans, what powerful connections they had in the political and business establishments, what clout they had in New Delhi, how they were able to manipulate the stock market, who their clients were, and which of them were able to sell the securities before the racket was discovered—these and scores of other questions were still being investigated when, in June, 1993, Harshad Mehta implicated in his scam Prime Minister Rao him-self. Mehta called a press conference with a lot of fanfare and announced that on November 4, 1991, he, his brother Ashwin Mehta, and two other men had carried to the official residence of the Prime Minister a suitcase stuffed with six million seven hun-dred thousand rupees—about two hundred and seventy-three thousand dollars—and handed it over for "political patronage and blessings" to the Prime Minister, who had thereupon entrusted it to his personal secretary, R. K. Khandekar. (Corporate contributions to political campaigns are, of course, illegal in India.) Mehta said that he would offer proof of the transaction if he was granted immunity from prosecution.

It is generally not possible to get Indian currency in notes larger than a hundred rupees, so Mehta would have had to pack at least sixty-seven thousand individual notes in his suitcase. The statement therefore seemed preposterous on the face of it. But over the years the Congress Indira's reputation had been so sullied that, although the charge was vigorously denied by the Prime Minister, there was a clamor in the national press for Mehta to be granted immunity and for Rao to step down until the charge was investigated. An editorial in the *Statesman* was one of many in the national press arguing for immunity:

> What he is entitled to, however, is immunity from prosecution on the well-understood principle that he is in a position to lead the investigators to the big sharks who have so far succeeded in remaining in the shadows. The Government is plainly on trial. If it does not come to a proper arrangement with Harshad Mehta it will not be able to escape the odium that it is fully behind the big crooks and wishes to protect them. It is already under strong suspicion that it has gone out of its way to protect the guilty in the Bofors scandal. Its reputation is unlikely to survive the charge that by a combination of sophistry and legal quibbling, it is refusing to accept assistance in unravelling the mystery that surrounds the largest fraud in the country's history.

Mehta was represented in various inquiries soon afoot by the formidable lawyer Ram Jethmalani and his son Mahesh; Ram Jethmalani had spattered Rajiv Gandhi with mud over the Bofors scandal, a cause of Congress Indira's defeat in the 1989 election. Opposition parties hoped that the securities scandal and Jethmalani would have the same effect on the fortunes of Rao and his government in the next election.

Rajiv Gandhi and Rama's Kingdom

There was confusion and uncertainty in government quarters even in the conduct of external affairs—an area in which there had formerly been a consensus. After Indira Gandhi came to office, India had acted like an important regional power—training militants from East Pakistan, arming guerrillas from Sri Lanka, subverting and taking over the Protectorate of Sikkim, bringing Nepal to heel with an economic boycott, refusing to come to terms with Bangladesh over river waters—but the day of reckoning was at hand. In addition, the end of the Cold War meant that India could no longer cynically play off the Soviet Union against the United States, getting, for instance, arms from one and food and technology from the other—a form of realpolitik that was the true basis of much of India's foreign policy, notwithstanding the government's profession of striving to maintain moral neutrality between the capitalist and the Communist camps. Nor could India any longer look to the Soviet Union as an economic model for the country's development. In fact, India was now much like the former Soviet Union in being economically at sea: the financial condition of the country was grimmer than ever before.

Among other things, weak governments had taken their economic toll. In the space of less than two years, from November, 1989, to June, 1991, India had had four Prime Ministers—Rajiv Gandhi, V. P. Singh, Chandra Shekhar, and P. V. Narasimha Rao. When Rao became Prime Minister, inflation was running at fourteen per cent; the budgetary process was out of kilter; foreign reserves were exhausted; India, with outstanding foreign debts of seventy-one billion dollars, was the third-largest debtor nation in the developing world, after Brazil and Mexico; and, for the first time, it was in danger of defaulting on its debts. To tide the country over, Rao's government sought an emergency loan from the International Monetary Fund. (A standby loan of two billion two hundred million dollars was eventually approved.) In the meantime, to attract foreign capital, the government instituted a series of economic measures that permitted multinational corporations to control Indian companies by allowing such a corporation to hold fifty-one per cent of the stock of its Indian subsidiary. Until then, multinational corporations had been restricted to forty-per-cent ownership. (In 1977, when that restriction was applied without exception, not only Coca-Cola but also I.B.M. chose to pull out of India rather than surrender majority interest in their subsidiaries. Only with a controlling interest, they felt, could they make Indians privy to beverage formulas, say, or to computer patents.) The economic measures introduced by Rao's government also made direct foreign investment possible in thirty-four major Indian industries, among them transportation, food processing, tourism, and the manufacture of electrical equipment. Moreover, as a spur to foreign investors, the government devalued India's currency by twenty-two per cent. Measures like the devaluation needed only an executive order, but other measures required passage of Parliamentary bills. As had been expected, they ran into heavy political opposition—after all, the socialist consensus of almost half a century was being turned on its head—but, since no party wanted Rao's government to fall as a result of the vote (that might have precipitated a new general election), the bills got through the Parliament and became law.

The economic measures were an important step toward dismantling the socialist controls on the country's economy, and some of their effects were soon evident. By 1993, the rate of inflation had come down from fourteen per cent to seven per cent; foreign reserves had shot up from almost nothing to more than five billion dollars, and were expected to continue to grow rapidly, because Rao's government, in one of its boldest moves, made the rupee fully convertible for settling trade accounts; and India was able to service its foreign debt on time. All the same, it would be some years before the country could feel the full impact of the reforms, and anyway foreigners would need many more inducements to begin investing in India in a significant way.

Meanwhile, politicians of every stripe were busy exploiting religious differences and creating religious turmoil. In Assam, the Hindus were continuing to expel hundreds of thousands of Muslim immigrants who had streamed in unchecked from impoverished Bangladesh. In other parts of the northeast, the Nagas, the Mizos, and the Gurkhas had all had secessionist movements afoot for some time. In the east, the Jharkandis, in Jharkand—the tribal areas of Bihar, Orissa, and Madhya Pradesh—were asking for a homeland of their own. Government compromises struck with the Nagas, the Mizos, the Gurkhas, the Jharkandis, or whomever always seemed to break down eventually, with the result that the demands grew. In the northwest, the government had transformed Kashmir, with a predominantly Muslim population, into a virtual police state; in fact, the brutality of the military repression there from the late eighties on had no parallel in independent India. The killings by the military in Kashmir were ominously reminiscent of the killings by West Pakistan's military in East Pakistan in 1971, which had led to the breakup of Pakistan and the birth of Bangladesh. As a consequence, even the few Kashmiri Muslims who might have wanted to keep Kashmir in India were being driven into the movement for secession: they were opting either for independence or, because they knew they couldn't stay independent long, for joining Pakistan. The government had only itself to blame for now having all but physically lost Kashmir. It had alienated the moderates by jailing their leaders without even a semblance of due process, or, alternatively, by reducing them to puppets through political bribery, with the result that the Muslim population had turned extremist. And the extremists had always been able to carry out with impunity their campaign to join Pakistan, because of the easy escape routes to Pakistan-held areas of Kashmir. Also in the northwest, in Punjab, the ominous religious conflict was continuing between the Hindus and the Sikhs.

Since 1987, the government had administered Punjab from New Delhi, under President's Rule, but it was making no headway in restoring order to the state. The Sikh extremists carried on an unabated hit-and-run campaign against innocent civilians in trains and buses, in houses and huts. Legions of unemployed, seeing a chance for religious advancement and perhaps personal gain—through looting, say—rallied to the extremists' cause, while criminals used the general lawlessness as a cover for their own activities. Members of the government's paramilitary Border Security Force and of the state police regularly killed suspected extremists, but their ferocious policy of suppression seemed only to stoke the fires of violence. Then, on November 9, 1991, the central government posted as Director General of Police in Punjab a Sikh loyalist, Karan Pal Singh Gill, who had a formidable reputation for reëstablishing law and order in disaffected areas. The government, judging the conditions in the state unfit for elections, had repeatedly postponed the election scheduled for September, 1991, and had extended President's Rule there, but now, within a matter of a few weeks, Gill brought some semblance of authority to the state by savage use of the proverbial stick, whereupon the government announced the poll for February, 1992. Sikh extremists, who didn't want to coöperate in any way with the hated government, delivered an ultimatum to the Punjabis: they had to boycott the election; if anyone stood for the legislative assembly or voted for a candidate he would risk being killed. As a result, the candidates were few and far between, and on the election day only twenty-two per cent of the eligible voters turned out—a record low. The Congress Indira won by default with a mere ten per cent of the vote, obtaining eighty-seven out of a total of a hundred and seventeen seats in the legislative assembly, and was able to form a state government with the Sikh loyalist Beant Singh as chief minister. Gill, now backed by the elected government of Beant Singh, greatly increased the size of New Delhi's Border Security Force; equipped the police with automatic rifles and jeeps, and even with armored tractors, to use in pursuing suspects into the fields; and successfully sealed the border with Pakistan, so cutting off the supply of weapons to the extremists. On August 9, 1992, the police managed to hunt down and kill Sukhdev Singh Babbar, the last surviving major leader of the international movement for Khalistan. The extremists retaliated by killing policemen's relatives—sometimes whole families—who lived in remote villages and had taken no part in the conflict. The families of senior police officers could be constantly guarded, but the ordinary policemen had no recourse from attacks on their relatives. The effect of the extremists' campaign, not surprisingly, was to mobilize the police against them everywhere, and observers say that, as a consequence, the Beant Singh and Gill combination was apparently able to annihilate an entire generation of Sikh youths, who had been at the core of the extremist movement. In any event, the state soon saw a decline in violence: in 1992, twenty-five hundred and eighty-three civilians and officials were killed, compared with forty-seven hundred and sixty-eight in 1991. In fact, for the first time since the early eighties the state seemed to be experiencing the return of democracy and normal life. In contrast to the state election of February, 1992, seventy per cent of the electorate voted in municipal elections in September, and eighty-two per cent voted in village-council elections in January, 1993. Punjabis—naturally exuberant, garrulous, and high-spirited people—began again to venture out into city streets and village lanes after dark and to hold public functions, such as showy weddings. Since the summer of 1992, the outflow of refugees from the state has stopped; land prices have tripled; and a brisk trade in whiskey, chickens, and eggs—old favorites of well-to-do Punjabis—has resumed. It is too early to say, though, whether these changes are harbingers of the defeat of the Sikh secessionist movement or are a mere respite from it. In the past, the secessionist fires in different parts of India, even when they were banked down, had a tendency to flare up and spiral out of control. Observers have recently said that if the country doesn't find a looser federal structure, with political and economic autonomy for states and regions, there is a real danger to the survival of the Indian union.

9

The Mosque
and Rama's Kingdom

It has been said that the Muslim revolution in Iran that toppled the Shah and ushered in the rule of the mullahs was brought about by the availability of cheap audiocassettes and cassette players, because that made it possible for Ayatollah Khomeini, the religious leader and the Shah's hated enemy, to record and secretly circulate, even to the most distant corners of Iran, revolutionary messages inciting people to rise against their ruler "in the name of Allah and social justice." Some observers have seen a similar revolution in the making in India, and, unquestionably, a wave of Hindu revivalism has grown stronger since 1987, when the Ramayana ("Romance of Rama"), the most popular of all Hindu epics, was serialized on national television. The effect of such a revolution could be to topple the secular democratic state that has existed since Independence, and usher in the rule of Hindu zealots.

In the eighties, television in India grew so much in importance that it served as a complement to India's cinema industry, which produced more films than that of any other country in the world. The national television channel, Doordarshan, or Distant Holy Audience, was a powerful instrument; in many parts of the country, it was the only source of information for illiterate people. It was used mostly as a vehicle for government propaganda (it showed a lot of shots of the Prime Minister of the day) and for serving up noncontroversial inspirational fare. The serialized Ramayana was the most widely seen television program in India. Many who watched it were first-time television viewers, and became hooked on the Ramayana.

The Ramayana is the nearest thing to a sacred book that the Hindus have. It was composed by Valmiki around 300 B.C. and runs to some twenty-four thousand Sanskrit couplets. Today, most people know it in a popular Hindi translation done by Tulsidas in the sixteenth century. Every year, episodes from the Ramayana are enacted all across the country at religious festivals, and every child in India is familiar with the basic outline of the story, which tells of the trials and the exemplary lives of the god-prince Rama and his wife, Sita. Rama, who is regarded as an avatar of the Hindu god Vishnu, is the eldest son of Dasaratha, the ruler of the kingom of Ayodhya in ancient India. The king has three wives and many children. During a battle, he is gravely wounded, and one of his wives, Kaikeyi, saves his life. In gratitude, the king asks her to make two wishes, but she demurs. Later, when Rama, the rightful heir, is about to succeed his father, Kaikeyi makes her two wishes: that the king banish Rama from the kingdom for fourteen years and crown her son, Bharata, king instead. Rama and Sita go into exile in the forest, and the old king dies of a broken heart. Bharata refuses the throne, however, and sets off in search of Rama. He finds the rightful heir, but Rama refuses to return to the kingdom until he has completed his period of banishment. Bharata places Rama's wooden sandals on the throne and rules in his name. In exile, Rama faces his greatest trial: the abduction of Sita by the demon Ravana. She is carried off to the demon's island kingdom, Lanka (thought to be present-day Sri Lanka). Rama locates her with the help of the monkey god Hanuman; fights Ravana with Hanuman's army of monkeys; and is victorious. He is reunited with Sita, and, his period of exile being over, he and Sita triumphantly return to the kingdom now restored to him. He is finally crowned king, ushering in Rama Rajya. The story doesn't end there, however. It turns out that Sita is pregnant, and people gossip that she was seduced by Ravana. Although she is innocent, she is sent into exile in the forest. There she gives birth to twin sons, Luv and Kush. She brings them up in poverty in the forest, and when she is eventually reunited with Rama she calls upon Mother Earth to testify to her innocence. The earth thereupon parts under her feet and swallows her up.

The Ramayana was adapted for television, at the government's invitation, by Ramanand Sagar, a successful producer of Hindi films. Sagar's Ramayana was broadcast on a hundred and four Sunday mornings, each episode lasting a half hour or so. The screenplay was formulaic, with one-dimensional characterizations and declamatory dialogue. What was notable about the serial was its pageantry—sumptuous settings and bright-colored, shiny costumes. It was a mixture of soap opera and national mythology, designed to appeal to everyone, from teen-agers to old people.

The initial broadcasts of the Ramayana were so popular that the government immediately asked B. R. Chopra, one of the most celebrated commercial producers in the history of Indian cinema, to adapt another Hindu epic, the Mahabharata ("Great Epic of the Bharata Dynasty"), for television. The Mahabharata, in the form in which it has come down to us, is a compilation of numerous legends, didactic stories, and ethical and theological homilies; like the Ramayana, it is filled with heroic action. (The Bhagavad Gita, one of the philosophical segments of the Mahabharata, is almost as well known as the Ramayana.) It was compiled by Vyasa around 400 A.D. and runs to some hundred thousand Sanskrit couplets, which make it about seven times the length of the Iliad and the Odyssey put together; in a modern Hindi translation, it takes up some five thousand printed pages. (P. Lal, a Sanskrit scholar and professor of English at the University of Calcutta, has been working on an English translation of the poem for many years, doing about twenty couplets a day.) The Mahabharata tells of a dynastic struggle between two branches of a royal family, the Bharatas, who supposedly lived between 1400 and 1000 B.C. One branch, the Kauravas, is the progeny of the blind prince Dhrtarastra; the other branch, the Pandavas, is the progeny of Dhrtarastra's younger brother, Pandu.

Although Dhrtarastra is the rightful heir to the throne, he is passed over, because of his blindness, and Pandu becomes king. When Pandu dies, at an early age, Dhrtarastra succeeds to the throne after all. Their sons carry on a feud, and it continues for generations. In the course of the narrative, five brothers marry one woman; a god turns up in the guise of a dog; the Pandavas lose their kingdom in a fateful throw of dice and are banished, retiring into the forest for thirteen years. There is a climactic battle, in which Krishna—who, like Rama, is popularly regarded as an avatar of Vishnu—is a participant. The epic ends with an arduous journey by the Pandavas to the gates of Heaven.

Chopra made ninety-three hour-long television episodes of the epic. They were broadcast between October of 1988 and July of 1990—on Sunday mornings, like the Ramayana. Much was made of illegitimate births, abductions of beautiful women, and treacherous goings on. Every ingredient of life, it seemed, was thrown into the pot. The serial is said to have been the most popular soap opera ever made. Chopra boasts that it had the most viewers of any serial ever produced anywhere in the world—that ninety-two per cent of the Indian viewing public saw most of it. Independent observers have estimated that eighty-five per cent of the viewing public saw all ninety-three episodes. And those figures do not include the people all over the world who have seen it on videocassette. The Mahabharata was shown on television in Great Britain. (The Peter Brook version of the Mahabharata, which was shown on public television in America, had nothing to do with Chopra's extravaganza.)

It is said that during the broadcasts of each epic serial the whole country came to a virtual standstill. Taxis, bicycles, and rickshaws disappeared from the streets. Telephones stopped ringing. Prayers and cremation rites were postponed. Ministers, civil servants, housewives, shopkeepers, hawkers, prisoners, water carriers, sweepers, scavengers—all dropped whatever they were doing to watch a screen in someone's house or in the village square. People who didn't have a television would often gather by the window of a house where people were watching the serial, so that they could watch or, at least, listen.

The two epics cast considerable light on the evolution of Hinduism from 400 B.C. to 200 A.D. And, though the Ramayana and the Mahabharata do not have the status of Scripture, some Hindus regard them as sacred and believe that there were gods and goddesses who actually lived in the world. This belief has been reinforced by television. Many viewers watching the epics responded as if they were worshipping at a temple. When Rama or Krishna—or another god—came on the screen, viewers might light a lamp in front of the screen and pray to it. The men who made the television epics and the players who acted in them were written about and venerated as devout people. They themselves claimed that they made the serials not for money—although, of course, a lot of money was made from them—but for devotional reasons.

While the serials opened the floodgates to a Hindu-revivalist tide, it was a tide that had been coming in since Independence: the years since 1947 have seen an attempt to emphasize the Sanskrit elements of written and spoken Hindi and an increase in the study of Sanskrit classics; a revival of ancient forms of dancing; a proliferation of societies to teach the Bhagavad Gita; the establishment of leagues to protect cows; the emergence of several hundred chauvinist holy men who claim to be reincarnations of gods and are worshipped as gods. Mahatma Gandhi and Nehru saw this tide approaching, and they tried to stem it by preaching and teaching secularism and by stressing Hindu-Muslim unity.

The resurgence of Hinduism and ancient Hindu values bore some resemblance to the fundamentalist movements among the Sikhs and the Muslims in India—and, indeed, among Muslims in Iran and other parts of the Middle East. Orthodox Hindus proudly declared that India was on the verge of Rama Rajya. They said that they had been sat upon by Muslims for three hundred years, during the Mogul rule, and by the British for a hundred years, during the Raj, and were finally about to come into their own. Many Hindu intellectuals defended the serials as an expression of Indic civilization and national culture, and defended Hindu "fundamentalism" as something very different from the fundamentalism of other religions, pointing out that Hindus had no holy book and no prophet; that, unlike Muslims and Christians, they didn't believe in one god or in proselytizing; and that Hinduism was more a way of life than a religion, since Hindus, as a rule, made no real distinction between the secular and the sacred.

Muslims, Sikhs, and Christians saw in the serials an attempt by the government to fill the airwaves with symbols of Hindu civilization and to drum up Hindu votes. Many of them feared for their way of life—perhaps with good reason, in view of the exponential growth of religious violence. There were demands for televised treatments of various non-Hindu texts. A Muslim historical drama, "The Sword of Tipu Sultan," based on the eighteenth-century leader Tipu Sultan, was broadcast in fifty-two installments; and, around the same time, filming of the Bible was begun in Kerala. (A fifth of Kerala's population is Christian, yet Kerala's voters had often voted Communist, and the Congress Indira Party initiated the project with the aim of courting the Christian vote. In the 1991 election, Kerala voted Congress Indira.)

Oddly, however, in 1991 the greatest television resources were being devoted to what was essentially a Buddhist story, although a Buddhist minority scarcely existed in India. Preparations were under way to film a narrative about Ashoka, who was an emperor of India in the third century B.C. Ashoka is not a religious figure on the scale of Rama or Krishna, but he went through a religious conversion to Buddhism (not unlike St. Paul's conversion to Christianity) and became a preëminent lay disciple of Buddha. His reign is remembered as the most enlightened and peaceful period in Indian history. The story of Ashoka was to be produced by Om Prakash Ralhan, who, though he was not so well known as Sagar or Chopra, had directed, acted in, and written screenplays for dozens of films. It was all to be filmed in what was called Ashoka City—a location created in a scrub area north of Bombay. In 1990, the Dalai Lama laid the cornerstone of the city, as a gesture of Buddhist support. Ralhan said that he was going to employ fifty thousand extras, ten thousand horses, and a thousand elephants, and that his show would outdo the previous serials, for it would employ top Western technicians, it would be filmed in both Hindi and English, and it would be dubbed in many languages. According to the publicity releases, it would be "the biggest," "the most expensive," "the most spectacular" show ever. Non-Hindus said that the making of the Ashoka story for the airwaves was only more Hindu propaganda, in that Ashoka and Buddha were born Hindus, and many Hindus regarded Buddhism as a reform movement within Hinduism. In any case, it seemed doubtful whether any of these later projects—still to be completed—would have anything like the impact of the Hindu serials. Congress Party members and other critics of the Bharatiya Janata Party linked the rise of the B.J.P. with the Hindu serials. Since 1987, its leaders had certainly exploited the religious mood that the serials created.

In the eyes of many people, the Bharatiya Janata Party was a political front for extremist, "Hindu first" social and paramilitary organizations, like the Rashtriya Swayamsevak Sangh and the Shiv Sena. The Bharatiya Janata Party's campaign, which caught fire after the broadcast of the Ramayana, laid the foundation for what might be permanent oppression of the Muslim minority. The most egregious example of Bharatiya Janata Party and Hindu extremism concerned a historic mosque called Babari Masjid, which was built in 1528, in Ayodhya, in what is now Uttar Pradesh, by a lieutenant of the Mogul Emperor Babar, who reigned from 1526 to 1530.

In 1987, the B.J.P., in concert with the R.S.S. and the Vishva Hindu Parishad (World Hindu Council), embarked on a campaign to demolish the mosque and erect in its place a temple to Rama. They called for the "liberation" of the mosque from the Muslims and for the establishment of Rama Rajya, the implication being that Rama Rajya would represent the second restoration of Ayodhya to Rama. The B.J.P. and its allies could not have chosen a more effective image and symbol than Rama to promote their cause among the people. For centuries, his exemplary life had been a model for Hindus, especially in Northern India. His name was known to every child and was constantly invoked as a symbol of love and peace, unselfishness and renunciation, suffering and endurance. Reciting "Rama" or "Ram" ("Ram" is the Hindi form of the Sanskrit "Rama") was to most Hindus a little like what making the sign of the cross is to Catholics. Although only the town of Ayodhya was associated with Rama, the B.J.P. and its allies claimed, on the strength of some dubious legendary sources, that the site of the mosque was the Ramajanmabhoomi (Birthplace of Rama). One bit of evidence buttressing their claim was that the mosque was next to the old Hanumangarhi (Hanuman Temple)— Hanuman being the god most closely associated with Rama.

The campaign of the B.J.P. and its allies was immediately seen by the Indian Muslims as a Hindu attack on their religion and their rights, and the preservation of the mosque became for them a symbol of their survival. At least since the time of the Great Mutiny of 1857, Hindus and Muslims of Ayodhya had been engaged in a legal tussle over the mosque in the British courts and, after Independence, in India's court system. In 1949, Hindus of Ayodhya surreptitiously introduced idols of Rama into the mosque, as if they intended to take the matter into their own hands now that India was independent. Idolatry in any form was anathema to Muslims, and the fact that the idols were Hindu added insult to injury. The new Indian government in the state, in order to avoid a Hindu-Muslim clash, declared the premises of the mosque a disputed area and locked the gates—without, however, removing the idols. Then began a legal wrangle of suits and countersuits, appeals and counterappeals—a sort of religious version of the Dickensian legal case of Jarndyce and Jarndyce—with the Hindus seeking to keep the idols in place, and the Muslims trying to have them removed and to regain possession of their mosque.

The handling of the case was a stock Indian response to an insoluble problem: to allow confusion, delay, and neglect to run their course, in the hope that one day a compromise would emerge.

In 1984, the Vishva Hindu Parishad, in Delhi, called for the "liberation" of the Ramajanmabhoomi from the Muslims and planned a week-long Rath-Yatra (Chariot Procession) from the neighboring state of Bihar to Ayodhya. The plans were aborted by Mrs. Gandhi's assassination. At the beginning of 1986, the Hindus increased their demands: they called for the construction of a temple to Rama on the site of the mosque. That demand was eagerly picked up and supported by the B.J.P. Meanwhile, Muslims started holding nationwide protests of their own, and demanding, in their turn, the "liberation" of the mosque, so that they could pray there; their calls became more strident after February of 1986, when a district judge ordered that Hindus be allowed to worship there. But the B.J.P. and its allies only intensified their campaign, whipping up Hindu sentiment and rallying people, most of them in Northern India, to their cause. On September 30, 1989, the Vishva Hindu Parishad organized a Shila Puja (Consecration of Temple Bricks). In each Indian village with a population of two thousand or more—the participating villages numbered some two hundred thousand—a brick was consecrated, and stamped "Shri Rama" ("Respected Rama"). Some of the bricks were then carried by volunteers to Ayodhya, and on November 9th the foundation was laid for a temple to Rama, the plinth only a hundred and ninety-two feet away from the mosque. The Janata Dal government of V. P. Singh stopped work on the temple, and in subsequent months it tried to bring the leaders of all the groups together, but failed. The following October, the B.J.P. finally began a Rath-Yatra—this time from Somnath, a town in Gujarat, to Ayodhya, nearly a thousand miles away. The B.J.P. succeeded in mobilizing tens of thousands of volunteers from all over the country to converge on Ayodhya. L. K. Advani, the leader of the B.J.P., rode in a motorized chariot, much as the Ramayana and the Mahabharata heroes did on television, and many of his followers dressed in costumes like the ones in the serials. Carrying bows and arrows, they tried to storm the mosque.

V. P. Singh's government, fearing Hindu-Muslim riots in the state and beyond, garrisoned Ayodhya with huge security forces, and the Hindu zealots were beaten back by tear gas and by shooting. A few people were killed and many injured. Although the government technically thwarted the goal of the B.J.P. Rath-Yatra, the Party's cause received enormous national publicity. After the great upset in the election of 1991, the B.J.P. was in a position to do what it liked in Ayodhya. Though the Indian Supreme Court was still in the process of adjudicating the question of whether the land on which the mosque stood belonged to the Hindus or the Muslims, the B.J.P. and its allies organized a second march on Ayodhya for December 6, 1992, this time with the ostensible purpose of building a platform for the temple on the foundation they had laid during the Shila Puja; as its leaders put it, the marchers would be "performing prayers with shovels and bricks."

In preparation for the event, the B.J.P. government of Uttar Pradesh constructed approach roads to the town, installed electrical connections, sanctioned money for sanitation and cleaning, and, through a fraudulent legal maneuver, acquired a 2.77-acre plot of land near the mosque, which included the gate and part of the boundary wall of the mosque's outer courtyard, and an adjoining Muslim cemetery. On the appointed morning, a quarter of a million people gathered in Ayodhya. Fifty or sixty thousand marchers thronged around barricades cordoning off the mosque. They were led in prayers and were addressed by senior leaders of the Vishva Hindu Parishad and the B.J.P. Around noon, about a hundred and fifty marchers broke through the barricades and, climbing up onto the domes and using primitive tools, such as sledgehammers, set to work smashing the mosque. Others began clearing the surrounding land by demolishing the houses of Muslims, who could offer no resistance.

Advani had given assurances to Prime Minister Rao that the marchers would not harm the mosque, and Rao had accepted the assurances, either because he thought that if something happened to the mosque blame would be attached to the B.J.P.—both its national leadership and its state government—or, more likely, because he was an indecisive man, who preferred to do nothing. (It was said that when he was a guest he had trouble deciding whether to drink coffee or tea.) In any event, he had not posted troops at the mosque. State police were present, but they did little more than set off a few rounds of tear gas and charge into the crowds with bamboo staves. Then the local administrators sent a "panic message" to the state authorities in Lucknow, the capital of Uttar Pradesh, and those authorities instructed the district magistrate in Ayodhyah to mobilize the Central Reserve Police Force, stationed outside the precincts of the town. But roadblocks that had been set up to control the crowds prevented the reinforcements from reaching the scene.

The leaders of the march, after making what eyewitnesses described as "feeble efforts" to stop the demolition of the mosque, sat silent and watched as the vandals methodically pulled it down. Within thirty-six hours, the structure had been razed to the ground, its debris whisked away, a makeshift temple erected, and an idol of Rama set up inside. The vandals and their leaders were such a well-trained band and did their work with such dispatch that it was hard to escape the conclusion that the entire operation had been planned.

On the face of it, the destruction of one mosque might not seem likely to have long-term consequences. Moreover, Babari Masjid had been of no particular architectural distinction and, because of the bitter controversy between Hindus and Muslims, had not been used as a place of worship for more than forty years and had been crumbling. Anyway, every village or town with a significant Muslim population had a mosque. But over the years Babari Masjid had become a symbol of the Indian government's determination to protect the Muslim minority and uphold the tradition of the secular state. India had a long history of maintaining amicable relations among its many religions; for instance, the sixteenth-century Mogul Emperor Akbar was renowned for his policy of impartiality toward and conciliation of all religions. Every leader of independent India had known that neither democracy nor the Indian Union could survive without a national policy of religious toleration.

The mosque's destruction touched off the most widespread Hindu-Muslim riots since the Partition. More than three thousand people were killed and more than a hundred cities had to impose dusk-to-dawn curfews. It was originally thought that the mosque was an issue only among the illiterate poor, and that middle-class people living in the cities would have no part in the religious conflict. But then, in January, 1993, what appeared to be organized gangs of Hindu hooligans staged riots and vandalized property in certain Muslim areas of Bombay, the commercial capital of India, in order to frighten and disperse the city's substantial Muslim population to the point where Muslim property could be picked up at depressed prices. Hundreds of Muslims were killed, and many middle-class Muslims did indeed abandon their land, shops, or houses to go and live elsewhere. Apparently in retaliation, the Muslim underworld set off bomb blasts in Bombay in March, compounding the casualties and property damage—this time of Hindus—many times over. In fact, Bombay was all but shut down by the worst religious riots it had ever known. An order to troops to shoot at sight in the city did not bring calm, and people there were asking for a declaration of martial law. Another result of the destruction of the mosque was a further weakening of India's feeblest government since Independence. An internal struggle for power in Rao's government had been under way for some months. Back in December of 1992, Prime Minister Rao was forced by the powerful Congress Indira Party boss Arjun Singh, who was then the Minister of Human Resource Development, to dismiss the B.J.P. government not only in Uttar Pradesh but also in Rajasthan, Madhya Pradesh, and Himachal Pradesh—the four northern states where it had been duly elected, and where nearly a third of India's population lives—and to institute President's Rule and arrest the Party's national leaders. The *Statesman* noted, "The cavalier treatment of federal principles leaves a vast stretch of North India without a popular government and the consequences will be no different from what they have been in other States where [President's Rule] has become identified with bureacratic misrule." Although the leaders were later freed, the belated and seemingly vindictive action against the B.J.P. unstrung India's government still further. In February, 1993, however, Rao did show enough resolve to prevent the B.J.P. from holding a big political rally in New Delhi. One reason he was able to take such action was that the B.J.P. relied for support on only a few states, and therefore had to show some restraint and responsibility if it was to have any hope of getting a national constituency and winning a general election.

With the destruction of Babari Masjid, mob rule was allowed to supersede the rule of the law. The B.J.P. and its allies took to claiming that Hindu temples once stood on the sites of other mosques besides Babari Masjid—in Mathura and Benares, for instance. Some hotheads even extended that claim to the Jama Masjid, in Delhi, which was perhaps the greatest mosque in India, and also to the Taj Mahal; indeed, the authorities were reported to be considering surrounding the latter, a "wonder of the world," with barbed wire. The hotheads produced little evidence to buttress their various claims. One could only ask how far, and to what effect, they would carry the process of erasing hundreds of years of the Mogul past from the palimpsest of Indian history in the hope of discovering Hindu glory. The Hindu campaign was superficially reminiscent of the Indian nationalists' replacement of British names of Indian streets with Hindu and Muslim names after Independence. But that had involved merely a change of street signs, and today people use the British and the Indian names interchangeably. The new Hindu campaign was seen as giving justification both to the Hindu faithful for taking the law into their own hands in the service of a higher purpose and to the Hindu politicians for capitalizing on the firestorm started by the destruction of the mosque. Certainly politicians had succeeded in making "Rama" a battle cry and turning a symbol of peace and renunciation of regal prerogatives into a symbol of violence and greed for power. Muslim militants had always used "Allah" as a battle cry—it was part of Islam's military inheritance—but the use of a god's name as a battle cry had no precedent in Hinduism, which had always been singular among religions in its reverence for all living things, the brutality of the caste system notwithstanding. Also, unlike the Muslims and the Sikhs, whose divines had always been involved in politics, as behooved theocratic religions, Hindu divines had traditionally stayed out of politics, because they had no one set of beliefs. Now, thanks to the Hindu extremists, Hindu priests had entered politics, and some of them were calling for a revision of the constitution in order to establish a wholly Hindu India—an India where Hindus, who made up eighty-three per cent of the population, would rule, and religious minorities (the Muslims, constituting eleven per cent; the Christians, constituting three per cent; and the Sikhs, constituting two per cent) would be reduced to second-class status. If one directed those priests' attention to the example of Lebanon, they looked blank. Either they hadn't heard of the country or they didn't think that what had happened in Lebanon could happen in India. One detected all across India a new feeling of uncertainty and religious instability, and also a general hardening of mood among Hindus, Muslims, and Sikhs, without any comprehension of the degree of social upheaval it augured. There was an unofficial report that in Kanpur, a big industrial city not far from Ayodhya, Muslims were being taken from their houses and tenements by the authorities, herded into a park, and, for their own protection, surrounded by police. Such operations were not generally reported in newspapers, and one could only wonder where else such things were happening. (Official information was often inaccurate and unreliable, for the government was constantly trying to keep inflammatory news out of the press, lest disturbances blaze through a country filled with antagonistic castes, tribes, and religious groups.)

The mosque episode raised anew the whole issue of Indian identity. In the old secular climate, people tended to think of themselves as Indians first; in the new climate, they were starting to think of themselves as Hindus, Muslims, or Sikhs first. Even some enlightened, liberal Hindus were starting to think of themselves as Hindus first, and jumped onto the B.J.P. bandwagon in the hope of bringing about the transformation of secular India into Hindu India. Thanks to religious passions inflamed by the B.J.P., the Hindu right and the promoters of religious bigotry seemed to be winning support from the secular centrists and the advocates of religious toleration. One could only wonder what fate awaited an Indian democracy in which a national political party brazenly appealed to religious passions for political gain. Just as India was finally freeing its economy from socialist shibboleths and government controls in preparation for joining the global economy, it seemed to be culturally regressing into pre-Mogul, medieval Hindu India; its response to rapid change seemed to be atavistic retreat. In a smaller country or a country with a more uniform religious character, the failure to resolve such a conflict between the new and the old might not be catastrophic. India, however, was all but a subcontinent, and its total Muslim population, of a hundred and ten million, was said to be higher than that of any Muslim nation except Indonesia.

It should be said that the Indian Muslims had to share the blame for the growing religious conflict. Since Independence, some of their well-known leaders, like Imam Bukhari and Syed Shahabuddin, had taken a conservative, almost fundamentalist line (the Muslim stand on the alimony of Shah Bano Begum was typical) and had done nothing to encourage open-mindedness and coöperation with Hindus and Sikhs. They had also done very little to improve the status of their people, who, by and large, were less well off economically than either the Hindus or the Sikhs. Hindu leaders, for their part, had never accepted the so-called Two-Nation Theory, which held that Islam was a nation and that Hindus and Muslims must have separate countries. They had long feared a pan-Islamic movement stretching from Pakistan through Afghanistan and Iran and across the whole of North Africa, and were delighted to have their own country's Muslims on the run. In a country whose religious minorities included—besides Muslims, Christians, and Sikhs—Parsis, Jains, Buddhists, and Jews, and which had already been partitioned, a struggle like that in Ayodhya over the mosque and the temple inevitably raised the spectre not only of Lebanon but also of Yugoslavia. Balkanization had all along been the greatest threat to India—for India, like the doomed Austro-Hungarian Empire, had many warring races, nationalities, and language groups. Only religious loyalties had ever united the villages and the cities, the poor and the rich. But the cohesive force that religion had once provided was now dissolving with the resurgence of fundamentalism and extremism in the dominant religions, and the attendant reactionism, fascism, and intolerance.

In late November and early December, 1993, however, new elections were held in the four northern states in which Rao had dismissed the B.J.P. governments the year before, and, even though the B.J.P.'s share of the popular vote did not decline, the Party was defeated in three of them, including Uttar Pradesh. A number of political analysts who had all along been confidently predicting its victory were quick off the mark with explanations: with the destruction of the Babari Masjid, the B.J.P. had lost its main rallying cry, and perhaps even its raison d'être; in recent years, voters had made a habit of throwing out the party in office; the voters had become disenchanted with the performance of B.J.P. governments; the B.J.P. governments had antagonized voters by cutting back expenditures on literacy, birth control, roads, water, and electricity, because the B.J.P. focus was not on development projects but on things like rewriting schoolbooks to extol the glories of Hindu India and of ancient Sanskrit texts; the voters were afraid of further religious violence; the fiery B.J.P. campaign rhetoric bore little relation to food, prices, and unemployment, which were the basic concerns of the poor; the voters were so sophisticated that they had seen through the religious cant of the B.J.P.; the B.J.P. had become a political pariah, and no other party would form an electoral alliance with it; the B.J.P. had peaked too soon; the B.J.P. had failed to shed its "upper caste" image; the B.J.P. had failed to come up with a program that appealed to all sections of a fractured, caste-ridden society; the B.J.P. had failed to bridge the gap between its economic interests and social aspirations and those of the lower castes and the Untouchables; in Uttar Pradesh, where Muslims had joined the lower castes and the Untouchables in tactical voting against the B.J.P., low-caste Hindus had created a new power center by forging an alliance with the Untouchables against the upper castes, the backbone of the B.J.P.; Congress Indira, which had captured power in two of the four states and lost narrowly in a third, turned out to have more life than anyone had expected; and so on. The political analysts were busy writing obituaries of the B.J.P. as a national party. But it has to be remembered that in 1977, when Mrs. Gandhi and her party were overwhelmingly defeated by the Janata Party, political analysts had written her off as a has-been who would never hold an office again; then, in less than three years, she was back in the saddle, and thereafter she and Rajiv ruled the country for almost nine years. The B.J.P., for its part, is taking heart from the fact that in an election in Delhi for the assembly of the National Capital Region—held at the same time as the state elections—it won fifty-three out of seventy seats, to the Congress Indira's fourteen.

Even if India did not disintegrate, the fact that for forty-five years of Independence the governments of Jawaharlal Nehru, Indira Gandhi, and Rajiv Gandhi had not succeeded in getting their priorities straight—had not minimized expenditure on defense in order to concentrate instead on hygiene and sanitation, on controlling the growth of population (since Independence the population had almost tripled) and the spread of pollution (New Delhi was now the third-worst polluted city in the world, after Mexico

City and Tokyo), and, at the same time, on extirpating illiteracy, liberating the Indian economy, and opening it up to foreign capital—meant that the country had forfeited a singular opportunity to modernize itself and to develop countervailing forces to religious extremism and Hindu chauvinism.

Cassandras, always highly vocal in India, have lately been saying that only some kind of dictatorship could preserve the unity of the country, and have predicted that sooner or later it will succumb to such a system, as so many of its poor neighbors have done. One could argue, however, that Indians are resilient people and have a way of living with their problems; hence John Kenneth Galbraith's description of independent India as a "functioning anarchy." And it may be that the extremely rigid hierarchy of three thousand or more castes and subcastes in Hinduism—a hierarchy that, though it has always been a pernicious force throughout the society, has also been a source of stability for more than twenty-five hundred years—can play a part in keeping the country together. Castes have been such a dominant part of Indian society that even when some of its people were converted to Islam—and most of the original Indian Muslims were converts—they continued, like the Sikhs, to observe the social distinctions of the Hindu caste system. In a sense, Indian Muslims have much more in common with Indian Hindus than with the Muslims in the rest of the world. And, certainly, all Indians have much more in common than did, say, the people of the former Soviet Union. Moreover, Hinduism has been for most of its history a pacific and tolerant religion, accommodating everything from animism to Tantric exercises and mysticism. It has never proselytized. In many ways, its syncretism, its resignation (or stoicism), and its fatalism (or acceptance) may be better suited to modern life than the principles of Christianity or Islam or Sikhism. The country's democratic tradition, though it is relatively new, has served as a safety valve for every kind of national, religious, and caste rivalry. Consequently, while throughout history the ending of a dynasty has often brought turbulence, in India's case its democracy might well act to defuse the current unrest. In any event, the middle class, which was a tiny fraction of the population at Independence, may now amount to as much as twenty per cent, and it has a strong interest in the survival of a democratic, united India.

INDEX

Advani, L. K., 146, 177–78
Ahmed, Akbar (Dumpy), 7, 8, 19
Ahmed, Fakhruddin Ali, 42
Akali Dal, 37–38, 39, 47, 66, 67, 68, 122
Akbar, Emperor, 179–80
Ambani, Dhirubhai, 119–20
Amritsar, 48, 49, 52
Anand, Amteshwar, 2, 3, 4, 5
Anand, T. S., 3
Anand, Viren, 8
Anandpur Sahib resolutions, 38, 39–40, 66
Anderson, Warren, 86
Andhra Pradesh, elections in, 20–22
Angre, Sardar Sambhaji Chandroji, 5, 6, 11
Appu (Asian Games mascot), 29–30
Ashoka, 174–75
Asian Games, held in New Delhi, 23–31
Assam: elections in, 96; protest movement in, 44–47; religious turmoil in, 166
Ayodhya, 175–80

Babari Masjid, 175–80
Babbar, Sukhdev Singh, 167–68
Bachchan, Ajitabh, 121
Bachchan, Amitabh, 121, 138, 140
Badal, Prakash Singh, 67, 68
Banatwala, G. M., 95, 97
Bangladesh, 45
Barnala, Surjit Singh, 68
Basu, Jyoti, 124
Begum, Shah Bano, 93–95, 96, 97
Bengalis, in Assam, 44–47
Bentinck, Lord William, 97
Bhagavad Gita, 173
Bharatiya Janata Party (B.J.P.), 3, 5–6, 9, 144–46, 150, 156–57, 158; and Hindu revivalism, 175–85
Bhave, Vinoba, 17
Bhindranwale, Sant Jarnail Singh, 38, 44, 49, 50–51, 52, 67
Bhopal, accident at, 85–92
Bhopal Act, 89
Bihar, 154–55
B.J.P. See Bharatiya Janata Party

"Blossoms in the Dust: The Human Factor in Indian Development" (Nair), 81–83
Blue Star, Operation. *See* Operation Blue Star
Bofors unit of Nobel Industries Sweden AB, 127–29, 143
Bombay Dyeing, 120
Bombay Stock Exchange, 162
Brahmachari, Dhirendra, 2, 6
Brandt, Willy, 150
British press. *See* India
Brook, Peter, 172
Bukhari, Imam, 183

castes, 186
Castro, Fidel, 32
Chandigarh, 37, 40, 66, 68
Chandra, Jag Parvesh, 117
Charles, Prince, 150–51
Chopra, B. R., 171, 172
Congress Indira Party, 3–4, 152–53, 156; centenary of, 75; Maneka Gandhi's opposition to, 16–19; and Rajiv Gandhi, 75–77; Lucknow convention, 7
Congress Party, 3, 117
Cowell, Ruth, 16
Criminal Procedure Code of 1898, 94

Desai, Mararji, 25
Dhawan, R. K., 2
Doordarshan, 169
"dowry deaths," 14–15
Dowry Prohibition Act, 15
Dumpy. *See* Ahmed, Akbar
Dyer, Reginald, 48

East Punjab. *See* Punjab
Economist, The, 159–61

Fairfax Group, 120–21
Fazal, Agha, 95

Galbraith, John Kenneth, 186
Gandhi, Feroze, 70
Gandhi, Indira: and Asian Games, 23–25; and Assamese protesters, 45–47; assassination of, 55–56, 128; dissension with Maneka Gandhi, 1–14, 18; as Indian leader, 32–33, 158; opposition to, 21–22; press attacks on, 19; and Punjab, 48–50; and Sikhs, 38–39, 41–44, 47, 49–50, 51–56; Sri Lanka policy of, 151
Gandhi, Mahatma, 48, 53, 72, 133, 157, 173
Gandhi, Maneka, 143, 155; book about, 21; dissension with Indira Gandhi, 1–14; after expulsion from Prime Minister's house, 15–19; attends Lucknow convention, 1, 7–9; Sikhs in family background, 11–12
Gandhi, Priyanka, 5, 70, 72–73, 153
Gandhi, Rahul, 5, 70, 72–73, 153
Gandhi, Rajiv, 2, 4, 12, 17, 19, 43, 143; assassination of, 149–52; and aftermath of Bhopal accident, 91–92; and Congress Indira Party, 75–77; corruption in govern-

ment of, 125–30, 133–34,
141–42; early years of, 70;
economic policies of, 63, 79,
119, 160; funeral of, 153; as
Indira Gandhi's successor,
61–63; and Muslim personal
law, 95–99; political activities of, 20, 21, 22, 24, 70–
71; as Prime Minister, 72,
136–39, 158; as rival of Sanjay's friends, 7; and P. C.
Sethi, 109–10; and Sikhs,
64–69; and V. P. Singh,
120–21; and Zail Singh,
121–23, 134–36, 139
Gandhi, Sanjay, 1, 3, 4, 13, 16,
21, 43, 71, 80; corruption
under, 131; friends of, 7
Gandhi, Sonia Maino, 4, 70, 71,
152–53
Gandhi, Varun, 2, 8, 11
Gill, Karan Pal, 167, 168
Godse, Nathuram, 157
Goenka, Ramnath, 120, 124
Gorbachev, Mikhail, 119
Gujurat, 74
Gurumurthy, S., 120, 124

Hamlyn, Michael, 108
Haryana, 37, 66, 136–37
Hegde, Ramakrishna, 141
Hershman, Michael, 126, 129
Hindu marriage customs, 14–15,
97
Hindu reforms, 99
Hindu revivalism, 169–75; and
the Bharatiya Janata Party,
175–85
Hindus, 36; and Sikhs, 47, 50–
51, 56–58, 65, 68–69

Hitler, Adolf, 41–42
Howaldtswerke Deutsche Werft,
125
Hurd, Douglas, 151

India: affirmative-action programs in, 143–44; British
press perception of, 157–61;
castes in, 186; Communist
Party in, 155–56; corruption
in, 112–13, 125–30, 131–
34, 141–42, 161–63;
drought in, 115–17; eco-
nomic conservatism in, 78–
80; economic problems of,
159–61, 164–65; elections
in, 46, 67–68, 124–25,
134–41, 144–48, 154–57,
184–85; foreign policy of,
164–65; long-term problems
of, 141–42, 185–87; mar-
riage customs in, 14–15,
93–99; *perestroika* in, 119;
political parties in, 145–48;
poverty in, 79–83; Presi-
dent's role in, 123, 135; productivity in, 78; religious
turmoil in, 35–41, 166,
175–85, 186; telephone
problems in, 101–11; television in, 169–75
Indian Express, 5, 119–20, 124,
126–27
Indian National Congress Party, 3
Indraprastha Indoor Stadium,
26–28
International Monetary Fund,
164
Iran, 169
Iyer, V. Krishna, 136

Jain, Girilal, 121, 132
Jain, Janendra Kumar, 5, 6–7
Jallianwalla Bagh massacre, 48
Jana Sangh Party, 9
Janata Dal Socialists, 143, 145, 156, 177
Janata Party. *See* Bharatiya Janata Party
Jats, 37–38, 137
Jehanabad, 154
Jethmalani, Mahesh, 163
Jethmalani, Ram, 163
Jharkand, 166

Kanpur, 182
Karnataka, elections in, 20–22
Kashmir, 166
Kaunda, Kenneth D., 150
Keenan, John, 86
Khalistan, 168
Khalsa, 36, 40
Khan, Arif Muhammad, 95–96, 98, 137, 138
Khan, Mohammed Ahmed, 93–95
Khandekar, R. K., 163
Khanna, H. R., 43
Khanna, Rajesh, 145
Khatris, 37
Khomeini, Ayatollah, 169
Kranti Ranga Party, 21
Kumar, Sajjan, 154

Lal, Bansi, 137
Lal, Bhajan, 111
Lal, Devi, 137, 155
Lal, P., 171
Le Corbusier, 37
Liberation Tigers of Tamil Eelam. *See* Tamil Tigers

Lok Dal, 137
Longowal, Sant Harchand Singh, 39, 40, 44, 66, 67
Lucknow convention, 1, 7–9
Luytens, Sir Edwin, 43

Ma, Anandamayi, 6–7
Madhya Pradesh, 85, 93, 110, 156
Mahabharata, 171–73
Maken, Lalit, 61
marriage customs, 14–15, 93–99
Mazhabis, 37
Meerut, 154
Mehta, Ashwin, 162
Mehta, Harshad, 162–63
Mirdha, R. N., 110–11
Mukherjee, Pranab, 153
Mulroney, Brian, 150
Muslim personal law, 93–99
Muslims, oppression of, 175–84
Muslim Women's bill, 98

Nair, Kusum, 81–83
Natarajan, S., 126
Nehru, Arun, 97, 98, 137
Nehru, B. K., 80
Nehru, Jawaharlal, 24, 36, 99, 130, 158, 173
New Delhi, India: Asian Games in, 23–31; water supply in, 117–18; working conditions in, 27–28
Nyerere, Julius K., 150

Official Congress Party, 3
Old Congress Party, 3–4
Operation Blue Star, 49–54, 65
Ortega, Daniel, 150

Palme, Olof, 128
Patnaik, J. B., 112
Pawar, Sharad, 156, 162
Prasad, Sharada, 11–12
Punjab, 74; election in, 155;
    Sikhs in, 36–37, 47, 48–50,
    66, 67–69, 167–68
Pure Drinks Company, 16

Raj, 157–58
Rajasthan, 116
Rajdhani General Traders, 13
Ralhan, Om Prakash, 174–75
Ram, Hardwar, 82
Ramachandran, M. G., 22
Ramayana, 169–71
Rao, Gundu, 20
Rao, Nandamuri Taraka Rama,
    21–22
Rao, P. V. Narasimha, 52, 152–
    53; as Prime Minister, 156,
    162–63, 164, 178, 180–81
Rashtriya Sanjay Manch, 18–19
Rashtriya Swayamsevak Sangh
    (R.S.S.), 5, 9, 175
Reagan, Ronald, 19–20
Rosencranz, Armin, 89
Rowlatt Act, 48
R.S.S. *See* Rashtriya Swayamsevak
    Sangh

Sagar, Ramanand, 171
Sathe, Vasant, 77–78
Scindia, Madhavrao, 6
Scindia, Rajmata Vijaya Raje,
    5–6
Scindia, Vasundhara, 6, 7
Sethi, Prakash Chand, 104–8,
    109–12
Shackle, Christopher, 50

Shahabuddin, Syed, 183
Shankaranand, B., 136
Shastri, Lal Bahadur, 140
Shastri, Sunil, 140
Shekhar, Chandra, 141, 144–45,
    158
Shiv Sena, 157, 175
Shourie, Arun, 73–74, 95–96,
    97, 124, 130
Shukla, V. C., 137, 138
Sikhs, 11–12; and Anandpur
    Sahib resolutions, 39–40; ex-
    tremists, 40–41, 49, 65,
    103, 166–67; and Indira
    Gandhi, 41–44, 47, 49–50,
    51–56; and Rajiv Gandhi,
    64–69; in Punjab, 36–37,
    47, 48–50, 66, 67–69, 167–
    68; quest for political power,
    35–39; relations with
    Hindus, 50–51, 56–58, 65,
    68–69; violence against, 56–
    58
Singh, Arjun, 88, 156, 180
Singh, Arun, 97, 98, 137–38
Singh, Beant, 167, 168
Singh, Charan, 25
Singh, Gobind, 36, 38
Singh, Joginder, 67
Singh, Khushwant, 68, 73
Singh, S. Nihal, 5
Singh, Vishwanath Pratap, 120,
    125–27, 132–33, 134, 135,
    136, 138, 139–40, 145,
    177; as Prime Minister, 143,
    158
Singh, Zail, 41–43, 139; and Ra-
    jiv Gandhi, 121–23, 134–
    36, 139
Sri Lanka, 151–52

Surya, 5–7
"Sword of Tipu Sultan, The," 174

Talwandi, Jagdev Singh, 39, 40
Tamil Nadu, 151
Tamil Tigers, 151–52
telephone system: problems with,
    101–11; strike at, 109–10
Telugu Nation Party, 21–22
Thackeray, Bal, 157
Thakkar, M. P., 122, 126
Thakkar Commission, 126, 129–
    30
Times of India, 121
Tohra, Gurcharan Singh, 67, 68
Tulsidas, 170
Tytler, Jagdish, 154

Union Carbide Corporation: acci-
    dent at Bhopal, 85–92

Untouchables, 144
Uttar Pradesh, 154, 156–57, 175

Vaidya, Arun S., 69
Valmiki, 170
Venkataraman, Ramaswamy, 136,
    137
Vishva Hindu Parishad, 175,
    177, 178

Wadia, Nusli, 120
wakfs, 98
Workmen's Compensation Act
    (Indian), 89–90

Yamuna River, 116
Yunus, Mohammed, 21

Zia-ul-Haq, Mohammed, 141

AFGHANISTAN
JAMMU AND KASHMIR
HIMACHAL PRADESH
Amritsar
PAKISTAN
PUNJAB
CHANDIGARH
Indus
HARYANA
DELHI
New Delhi
UTTAR PRA
RAJASTHAN
GUJARAT
MADHYA PRA
DAMAN & DIU
DADRA & NAGAR HAVELI
MAHARASHTRA
Bombay
ANDHRA PRADESH
GOA
ARABIAN SEA
KARNATAKA
Mad
Sriper
TAMIL NADU
KERALA
SRI LANKA
INDIAN